T0110555

THE ADAMS CHRONICLES:

VOLUME I

Hills of Appalachia
to a Kasbah in Morocco

LOUIS E. ADAMS

authorHOUSE®

AuthorHouse™
1663 Liberty Drive
Bloomington, IN 47403
www.authorhouse.com
Phone: 1 (800) 839-8640

© 2017 Louis E. Adams. All rights reserved.

No part of this book may be reproduced, stored in a retrieval system, or transmitted by any means without the written permission of the author.

Published by AuthorHouse 12/16/2016

ISBN: 978-1-4490-8855-2 (sc)
ISBN: 978-1-5246-5536-5 (e)

Library of Congress Control Number: 2016920922

Print information available on the last page.

Any people depicted in stock imagery provided by Thinkstock are models, and such images are being used for illustrative purposes only. Certain stock imagery © Thinkstock.

This book is printed on acid-free paper.

Because of the dynamic nature of the Internet, any web addresses or links contained in this book may have changed since publication and may no longer be valid. The views expressed in this work are solely those of the author and do not necessarily reflect the views of the publisher, and the publisher hereby disclaims any responsibility for them.

Acknowledgements

Copyright 2016 by Louis E. Adams. All rights reserved.

Acknowledgements, Credits and Privacy Issues Disclaimer: information contained herein represents the personal views of the author, and should not be assumed to reflect the official policies, procedures or practices of the United States Navy, the Peace Corps or any other government organization or agency.

I am grateful for the assistance and understanding of my wife, Shirley, the patient support of my cherished children, and the everlasting love of my grandchildren.

I have also benefited over the years from the friendship and collegial association with my good friend Ron Beathard, without whose genial encouragement and editorship this book may not have seen the light of day.

Every effort has been made to acknowledge the source of all statements and quoted material contained in this text, which is in the public domain, either through footnotes, narrative text, or endnotes, or in the reference section. The opinions expressed in this writing are exclusively those of the author and any contrary viewpoint awaits a challenge by the reader.

Any profit from the sale of this book will be donated to the Cystic Fibrosis Foundation (CFF) of Southwestern Ohio and the Children's Hospital in Cincinnati to assist in the much need research and treatment of all patients, like my grandson, Blake James Warren, who is a victim of this genetic disease.

Front Cover: Thanks to McKell Library, Ross County Historical Society, Chillicothe, Ohio for permission to use the scene of Mount Logan and the Scioto River.

*****

An Ode to my Mother

I would rather have one little rose
From the garden of a friend
Than to have the choicest flowers
When my stay on earth must end.

I would rather have one pleasant word
In kindness said to me
Than flattery when my heart is still
And life has ceased to be.

I would rather have a loving smile
From friends I know are true
Than tears shed around my casket
When this world I've bid adieu.

Bring me all your flowers today
Whether pink, or white, or red;
I'd rather have one blossom now
Than a truck load when I'm dead.

--Anonymous

Table of Contents

Acknowledgements: iii
Ode to Mother: v
Table of Contents: vii
Preface: ix
Introduction: xi

Chapter 1: The Well, the Pumpkin, and I. 1

Chapter 2: Roots, Strong Roots. 9

Chapter 3: Growing up in Down Times. 15

Chapter 4: Hopewell Saga & Reunions. 29

Chapter 5: Health Care............................. 39

Chapter 6: Gods, Goddesses, & Myths. 43

Chapter 7: Readin', Writin', & Chiggers. 53

Chapter 8: The Adams Farm. 59

Chapter 9: Village Smithy &
    Mathematician. 69

Chapter 10: Blizzard of 1950. 75

Chapter 11: Boys & Chickens or Eggs. 81

Chapter 12: Good Times & Bad Girls. 87

Chapter 13: Leaving for The Navy 97

Chapter 14: In the Navy. 105

Chapter 15: Hospital Corps School. 117

Chapter 16: Duty at Norfolk. 127

Chapter 17: Brothers Serve Together. 137

Chapter 18: Duty at Bethesda & Lejeune. .153

Chapter 19: On the Road to Morocco. 169

Chapter 20: I Slipped Burly Bonds
    of Earth 189

Chapter 21: Two Tragedies. 205

Chapter 22: Travels with Hiram Abiff. 211

Chapter 23: The Final Chapter. 221

Chapter 24: Out of the U.S. Navy. 225

Photographs and Captions 229

Addendum A: 235

Addendum B: 239

Addendum C: 241

Addendum D: 247

Addendum E .... .271

Addendum F 275

References .... .277

*****

Preface

You may ask why an eighty-year-old would want to write his autobiography. My life is approaching twilight, and I must consider that my past may have been of some small value. I write it down to preserve it from boorish and even vulgar forgetfulness, even my own. "Before the colors fade" is a phrase that comes to mind. I agree with Mark Twain [1] who wrote: "Age is an issue of mind over matter. If you don't mind, it doesn't matter."

Few people take the time to write about themselves. They expose themselves and are vulnerable to the risks of finding the real truths of life.

Therefore, not unlike prophets who are not without honor, except in their hometown, and among their own kin, or the Scot in his own house, I plunge headlong into this endeavor at some risk, agreeing with Sir Kingsley W. Amis [2]: "If you can't annoy somebody, there's little point in writing."

*****

Introduction

This journey begins with a young boy growing up during the Great Depression and World War II. He is a member of a large Scot-Irish folk, providing for their families before food stamps, Medicaid, and other social welfare programs existed. They worked a hilly, southeastern Ohio farm in the foothills of Appalachia.

These were anxious, and at times, fearful days following Pearl Harbor, the draft, the Korean Conflict, and the Cold War of the 1950's. Then came the 1960's: hope, anger, and war. It was a time of social revolution: The Viet Nam War, the Kennedy-Camelot years, the "Era of Nixon" (which represented some of the darkest hours of the 20th century), progress in civil rights, the Twist, and a man on the moon.

During the turbulent 1950's this young boy, now a young man, joined the United States Navy. And later, inspired by the words of President John F. Kennedy— "Don't ask what your country can do for you. Ask what you can do for your country"—became a member of the Peace Corps in Morocco.

This farm boy, led with the help and support of his wife and family, attended college, received a faculty appointment, and posted a long, academic career in the Department of Medicine at the University of Cincinnati.

Appalachian Ohio could be called the 51st state. The counties of southeastern Ohio are rugged and wooded—a land of hills and valleys. Its geography and history, its cities and small towns, and most of all, its people, are a wonderfully unique part of America. I am proud that Appalachia is part of my heritage.

Each family has its rich body of folklore they tell over and over. We never tire of hearing these stories, even when we know the ending. The telling is the meaning. Artist Norman Rockwell used a paintbrush; photographer Ansell Adams, used a camera; and we, the storytellers of Appalachia reveal our knack for capturing the simplest and most sentimental moments of everyday life with everyday words (3-5). We tell the stories so the listener can see them. This was an exceptional talent my mother possessed. Grandfather Elijah had it, as did many others. We people of the hills of Appalachia share the gift of storytelling.

What writer has not provided us with sound economic reasons for leaving this area during the Great Depression and post WW II, only to struggle to find the words to express why these same hills invariably call their children home to retire or to die? Perhaps not such a unique experience in nature, this yearning for a place to which one is somehow connected. After years in the vast ocean, salmon return to spawn in the same small stream from whence they and their forebears came; and, monarch butterflies make the journey from the eastern seaboard of the U.S. to the same field in Mexico that had been the birthplace of previous generations. Their journey there and back again is unchanging, but each generation makes the journey only once. Is it really so strange then that humans might feel some of this magnetism toward their native soil itself?

As for the dawn of this journey, my ancestors can thank King James I of England for sending the Scots to Northern Ireland before their eventual travel to America in the 1600s and their ultimate settlement in Appalachia.

We have a deep love for story-telling. In country stores, church picnics, on the front porch, by the fireplace or wood stove, memories and stories intermingle, merge, and become our way of life. It bonds us, those with Scot-Irish culture, into a community, into one deep, powerful, everlasting, and profound family.

Storytelling is like a can of worms. Stories wriggle around, going where circumstances allow, beginnings and ends merge, and the past becomes the future. The narrative becomes a form of identity and that's what makes stories good. Therefore, since the torch has been passed to my generation, it is with great humility that I attempt to carry on the tradition of storytelling. Here are some of our stories.

*****

CHAPTER 1

The Well, the Pumpkin, and I

When I was fifteen years old I fell into an abandoned well because of a pumpkin. The well was deep and I thought I was going to die. I experienced my life passing through my memory in that dark, damp hole. All the old stories came back.

Leisure time for a farm boy was limited to Saturday nights. On this particular evening, I was returning from the Circleville Pumpkin Show and decided to join my younger brothers who were camping with our hunting dogs back on the hill.

First held in 1903, the iconic Pumpkin Show started as a way for country folks to show off their produce to city slickers and to one another. The "Greatest Free Show on Earth" featured carnival rides, contests, and a lot of pumpkin-themed food, including pumpkin-burgers, fudge and taffy.

On my way to the campsite, climbing through a barbed-wire fence at the top of the first hill, I stopped to listen to the sound of barking dogs in a fox chase. The overcast night was still. The only sounds heard were from my own breathing and a faint sound from a house-dog barking nearby. My Levi's and old work-shoes were soaked from the grass and weeds wet from an earlier rainfall. I switched on my flashlight to check my watch, but the batteries were too weak for me to see anything. I wasn't worried because I knew the layout of the old farm like the back of my hand.

I began running down an old logging road. I knew my brothers, Bert and Ed, and our friend, Bob Tilton, had made camp in the back section of the farm near the base of Rattlesnake Knob. After racing through bramble briars and underbrush, I came upon an open field near a deep ravine and the old waterfall. Here, I stopped to listen for the hounds or the rushing of water passing over the falls. But there were no sounds of dogs or light from their campfire.

Walking towards the waterfall, I suddenly found myself falling forward and sliding down a steep embankment. After what seemed to be two or three minutes of uncontrolled downward movement, my body plummeted over the edge with a crushing impact into the deep water below.

I struggled to remain calm and study my situation. I realized that the lower half of my body was submerged in water. I tried to move my legs. There was no sensation in my left leg. My other limbs were alright, except for some pain in my right shoulder.

I slowly extended an arm to survey the dark surroundings. I felt the blunt ends of rocks protruding all around me. By feeling around, I could sketch a picture of my enclosure - a rock cylinder about four feet in diameter. Struggling to remain

2

upright, I realized I had fallen into the old abandoned well located near the waterfall.

Alone in darkness, perspiration - no, it was a cold sweat-- flowing down my forehead and across my face. I could taste the salt as it drained across my lips and into the corners of my mouth. My heart beat heavily, and I tried with all the strength I could muster, to overcome the fear of being trapped in the well. All my memories of the past seemed to flood my mind.

As time went by, the water became very cold and I felt pain in my left foot, hipbones, and shoulder blades. Minutes seemed like hours. I gathered strength enough to reach overhead and grab the edge of the rocks that lined the sides of the well. Climbing out by placing my feet on each side of the well, pulling my body upward by my hands, and clinging to the rocks overhead was my plan of escape.

Time after time I tried to gain a foothold on the wet, slippery rocks, but my efforts were useless. The job of climbing out of a well in this manner would not be easy for someone in good health, let alone for a person who had injuries.

I tried yelling for help. I cupped my hands around my mouth, faced up towards the opening, and yelled as loudly as I could. Surely my brothers must hear me calling! I waited. I yelled again. I waited. Then I knew. No one could hear my muffled calls from deep within a stone-lined well.

3

My body temperature was rapidly falling and I could feel the water-chill throughout my body. Pain in my left ankle was getting worse. I tried to get comfortable by shifting my weight and moving my feet in the mud and silt on the bottom of the old well. What if no one heard my calls for help? I could be trapped here overnight. Maybe days?

My head fell forward and I realized I had dozed off; for how long I didn't know. I raked the muddy strand of wet hair away from my eyes and saw a faint outline of my cold and wet hand. Turning my head skyward, I could make out the opening at the top of the well.

"The moon has come out from behind the clouds," I said to myself. It must be well past midnight. I called for help. "I'll keep yelling, or they may not find me."

Unknown to me, Bert and Ed had returned to the house around midnight because they had been unable to get the campfire started due to the wet wood. They discovered I was not in bed.

"That's a bit strange. I wonder what happened to him." Bert said.

"I don't know. He did say he would join us back on the hill after he got home; didn't he? Do you think he tried to find us and got lost?" Ed asked.

"No, he knows those woods too well to get lost," Bert answered. After a long silence, Ed asked, "By the way, did you notice how strange Old Jack was acting when we first got back? He just stood there at the end of his chain, whining, his ears up, and looking back over the hill...like he heard something."

"Do you think we should get the Jeep and drive back on top of the ridge and look for him?" Bert asked. He took the keys from a nail on the kitchen wall near the back door.

"Yes, and we'll take Old Jack with us too," Ed said, pulling his boots on over his damp socks.

Neither brother said anything as they drove to the top of the first hill. The good road was on this ridge. They could see Old Jack in the headlights about 20 feet ahead of them.

When they got to the fence leading into an open field along the ridge, they stopped the Jeep and got out to listen to the sounds of the night. The only noise they heard was a screech owl calling to his mate in the distance. Suddenly they heard Old Jack barking just ahead of them. Bert turned on the headlights of the Jeep and they noticed that the dog would bark, turn around and come back towards the Jeep, and then run forward again as if he were trying to get them to follow.

"He must hear something down towards the old waterfall, "Ed said. Bert started driving down an old logging road in that direction.

"Where did that damn dog go?" Bert asked, pulling the Jeep to a halt.

"He ran off that way...somewhere over there," Ed replied, aiming his finger off to the right side of the Jeep.

Bert shut off the engine and they climbed out of the Jeep. They could hear the dog barking ahead of them, in a hollow near the waterfall. They jumped back into the Jeep and raced across the uneven, wet field. Arriving at the rim of the deep hollow, they searched for the old road that would lead them near the falls.

Unable to find the road, they drove over some underbrush and wrangled around several trees until they were close enough to see Old Jack in their headlights.

"Sounds like he's barking down into that old abandoned well," Bert said.

They jumped out of the Jeep and ran down the steep hill stretching to the edge of the well.

"It's about time you got here," I yelled from my cold, wet tomb to the shadows overhead.

"What the hell are you doing down there? Are you okay?"

"I think so, except my foot. Do you have a rope or something you can us to pull me out?" I asked.

"Wait right there. We'll get another flashlight and the lantern from the Jeep so we can see what we're doing." Bert said.

"Don't worry, I'm not going anywhere. I am just so glad you guys found me," I yelled back, exhilarated.

"Good boy, Jack," Ed said, patting the dog on his head.

Moments later, the brothers returned to the well with a flashlight, lantern, and a log-chain. "We'll have to use this. I hope it's long enough to reach," Bert said as he lowered the chain into the well. "Here, Ed, you hold the light...I'll try to pull him out," Bert said as he got down on his knees and lowered the chain into the well. "Can you reach it?" he asked.

"Yes," I said as I grasped one of the links of the heavy chain.

"You can help by putting your feet on the edge of the rocks as we pull you up?" Bert suggested. He motioned for Ed to grab hold of the chain.

"I don't know how much help I can be. My left leg and foot really hurt, but I'll try." I said, trying to free my feet from the muddy quagmire.

Slowly, with both brothers pulling upward on the chain, I began my slow ascent from the well, escaping the cold, foul water that had been my home for more than four hours. At the top, on safe ground, I stood for a moment with my arms around the shoulders of my brothers as we stared down into the well.

"What is this floating on top of the water? It looks like a dead rabbit," Bert said, laughing.

After a quick examination of my leg, my brothers immobilized the foot and lower leg with a crude splint made from two pieces of lumber from the Jeep, and placed their belts around my leg to secure the splint in place for transport. With my sore arms around their necks, three jubilant brothers slowly sauntered back to the Jeep.

"I just knew you would come and get me out. But what happened to the campfire? Did you guys go hunting?" I asked.

"More important, how was your Pumpkin Show date with Ellen? Did you get any?" Bert inquired.

"What do you mean, did I get any?" I answered.

"Did you score? Did you get into her pants, or did you just play around with her," came the follow-up tease from Bert.

"No, I almost did. I would have if it hadn't been for her younger brother and sister being with us," was my lame response.

"Well, Big Brother, I guess I'll have to take her out next weekend and show you how it's done," Bert said teasingly.

"We never would have found you if it hadn't been for Jack," Ed said in a more reflective tone, as the old Jeep turned toward the house, with Jack trotting along in the headlights leading the way.

Memories of our youth are fleeting as a summer breeze; others linger in the deep deposits of our mind and are called forward in time of fear or wonderment.

*****

8

CHAPTER 2

Roots, Strong Roots

Our parents were born in eastern Kentucky in the early 1900's; Dad on Irish Creek in Lawrence County, near Blain, and Mom on Wiley Branch in neighboring Johnson County. In this area of Kentucky, folks were either farmers, worked in the timber industry, or were coal miners.

Few people in those days obtained a formal education. Dad dropped out of school at age thirteen to go to work and Mom had to quit school in the third grade because of a hearing defect due to childhood illness. However, they both had good common sense.

Our maternal Grandpa William "Pub" Daniels raised tobacco and sorghum cane for making sorghum molasses as cash crops. I remember he used a span of mules to pull a wagon in the hay field during cultivation in his tobacco patch; and, he used a single mule hitched to the end of a long pole that traveled in a circle to power the press that squeezed the juice from the sorghum cane that was collected and cooked or boiled-down later to make molasses.

He frequently reminded us that mules also played a vital role in the timber industry as an important economic factor in Johnson, Lawrence, and Pike counties until the late 1900's. Mules were used for skidding logs off hillsides and out of the hollows to large streams and into the Big

Sandy River, where they were floated down the river to a sawmill.

Other first, second, and third-generation relatives on both sides of the family worked cutting timber, in the tobacco fields, and deep inside the coal mines of eastern Kentucky, as did many other Scotch-Irish immigrants. They were a proud and resilient people, working the tough land, during tough times…a time when coal was_King. Both timber and coal were ripped from the mountains to fuel a growing nation.

Nonetheless, most of the prosperity from the timber and mineral rights ended up in the pockets of absentee owners. Unfortunately, these mountain people didn't realize the implications of their potential wealth. Many sold their timber and mineral rights for pennies on the acre to outlanders, who were strangers and did not live in the region.

In turn, they often became the laborers who built the roads and access routes to the timber, and to the coal mines under land they once owned; or, at the very best, they became coal-truck drivers rather than entrepreneurs. "You load sixteen tons and what do you get? Another day older and deeper in debt."

There is a legendary tale that captured our interest regardless of how many times is told. The tale about the first trip our Mother and Dad made together to Ohio in his Model "T" Ford Roadster, right after they were married on Christmas Day in 1933.

Mom and Dad met about six months earlier while she worked as a housekeeper for an elderly couple in Ashland, Kentucky. It was love at first sight for Dad; and, they were married by the Reverend Guy Preston in Paintsville, Kentucky. She was a young bride of 24 and Dad had just turned 21 in June that same year.

Mom was the third of eight children born to Mandy Elizabeth (Brooks) and William "Pub" Daniels [6,7]. According to Dad, "She was the pick of the litter."

Mom was given the Christian name "Iuka." She was the third of nine children born at home in a farmhouse near the towns of River and Lowmansville, Kentucky, in the Eastern Highlands deep in the heart of Appalachia. The name "Iuka," I learned later, was given to her by her father who had knowledge of a Choctaw Indian Chieftain called Iuka who lived in a village that later became known as Iuka in Mississippi. Her parents were also direct descendants of Hezekiah Sellards, [8] who was the father of the renowned Jenny Wiley who was captured by Indians).

Open discussions about our Dad's ancestry were infrequent and certainly less detailed in those early days. There had been an occasional remark made by our paternal Grandpa Elijah Adams at times when we children were being mischievous or naughty. He would invariably instruct us to "...act like somebody, because we had two Presidents in the family." Armed with this information we were expected to reform or change our behavior patterns. No explanation was made about the meaning of that statement.

We knew that our Dad was born in 1913 on a farm located somewhere on "Irish Creek," near Blaine in eastern Kentucky [6, 7]. He was the oldest of nine children born to Pearlie Jane, called Pearl, and Elijah Bert, often called Bert or just plain "Lige" by his friends. They were first cousins. Grandpa Adams, who died in1959, looked like a giant to me and it seems his hair was white very early in his life. Also, he always prayed or, as he called it, "turn thanks" before eating any meal.

Grandma Adams made buttermilk biscuits "from scratch" every morning. She didn't use a rolling pin but pinched off a piece of dough between her thumb and forefinger and patted the dough to make perfect biscuits that were all the same size when removed from the hot oven. There was cornbread for supper every night. It was "Kentucky Cornbread"; no sugar or eggs added. Grandpa always said he wanted cornbread not cake for supper!

From time to time we visited a few of our close relatives in Lawrence County, near Webbville, during yearly trips to Kentucky in the 1940's and early 1950's. But as children we never traveled to the mysterious "Irish Creek." Usually the first stop the old Model "A" Ford made over the short-cut route to Johnson County was on Kentucky Route #1 over to near Webbville for a brief stay with Aunt Hester Crabtree and her son Orville.

Aunt Hester was one of our grandfather Elijah's half-sisters. A peculiarity about Aunt Hester to us kids was that she smoked a corncob pipe and chewed tobacco. It was not store-bought tobacco; it was from Orville's "little patch" that he planted and harvested every year in the "bottom land" near the old log house. As boys, we also looked forward to sneaking away to the barn to see Orville's mules, Jake and Jack.

In Ohio, horses were commonly used in the fields, but mules were an important fixture on Kentucky farms from the time settlers began pouring through Cumberland Gap and even up until late in the 1960's. It used to be that you bred a skinny old donkey with a worn-out mare and hope to get a decent mule, Orville once told me. With the renewed interest in mules, we've been getting crosses with Clydesdales, Tennessee Walkers and all kinds of other things, he said later.

Our grandfather's other half-sister, Madeline (Wellman) Gallion, lived in Ashland in Boyd County, Kentucky. If time permitted, the family would also visit her and Uncle Bill on our way back to Ohio. No detailed information of other relatives was ever provided that I can remember.

It wasn't until late in the 1990's while researching genealogical history of the Adams family from Lawrence County Kentucky that I learned the names of my other many relatives [6,7]. It was then I discovered that my paternal grandparents,

13

Elijah and Pearlie Jane, had moved their family from Chattaroy, West Virginia to Ohio in 1925 [6,7].

This move came about because Elijah, at age 31, was in pursuit of finding a more reliable means of support for his growing family. During strikes in the coalmines, he and relatives had traveled to a rich farming area near Hallsville and Kingston, Ohio each fall of the year to cut corn. Demand for seasonal hired hands was great during that time of the year when the crops were being harvested. This move was an opportunity for Lige to return to the soil, as farming was deep-rooted in Adams' heritage [6,7]. **Figure #1**. Pearlie Jane and children at Logan Elm reunion in 1970. For general interest, **Figure #2** shows Earsel Adams Family in the 1980's

---

As noted, my ancestors were sharecroppers and coal miners - both low-paying, body-wearying occupations that vanished or offered diminished job security. But when coal started to go bust, after the interest in the new forms of clean energy, there were fewer jobs in the mines. There were no retraining programs available for those who had worked in the mines. The people affected were the next generation from those who welcomed LBJ's War on Poverty but now share the blue-collar sentiment that blames government and big business for their poverty, drug and alcohol addictions, violence and families in disarray. Sociologist, talking heads, poll takers, and political scientists have spent millions of words trying to explain how Donald Trump was elected President in 2016. Whether you agree with J.D. Vance or not, you must read his book "Hillbilly Elegy" [9] and thank him for bringing this thought provoking subject to the forefront.

*****

CHAPTER 3

Growing Up in Down Times.

The Great Depression (1929-39) was the deepest and longest-lasting economic downturn in the history of the Western industrialized world [10]. The year I was born, 1935, Ohio's unemployment rate was more than 37%. Millions of American workers lost their jobs. More than 40% of factory workers and 67% of construction workers were unemployed. Industrial workers, who were fortunate enough to keep their jobs, faced reduced hours and wages. They had a difficult time supporting their families. Many of Ohio's city residents moved to the countryside, where they hoped to grow enough food to feed their families.

We were a small family during that time, living on Charlie Spencer's farm. We did not own the farm. Dad was just a farmhand. The old, log-house on the farm was the "tenant house." It was an approximately 15' x 24' square hip-roof wooden structure built on a cinder block foundation with a small back porch extension. The wood-burning stove was in the middle of the living room and the chimney came out the middle of the roof.

The construction made it nearly impossible to heat the house because there was no insulation and the cold simply seeped into and settled in the walls, despite the addition of some plaster on the walls and ceilings throughout. The wood floor did not help ward off cold. The building contained three rooms, a kitchen-dining room, a living room, and a bedroom. This is where I was born on a cold and snowy night in February 1935.

Years later my Mother told me that the house was without electricity or running water. Water came from a deep-rooted cistern in front of the farmhouse that was filled with rain water through a system of house gutters from the tin roof. Household cooking and drinking water had to be collected at a natural spring and hauled by the bucket to the house. The soft rainwater garnered in the cistern was used for bathing and washing clothes.

The privy was unusually large. It was like most freestanding outhouses. It had two holes and a moderate-pitched shed roof with board-and-batten construction which helped blend the building with the house as well as declare the structure's intended longevity. Since we had no inside bathroom with running water, we kept a bucket or "chamber pot" under the bed at night.

In the mid-1940's, Dad was hired by the Mead Paper Company in Chillicothe, and over time he saved enough money to buy a deserted house with five acres of land on Walnut Creek Road. So, we moved to the uplands near Tucson and Moorsville. After clearing the overgrowth of weeds, running the blacksnakes out of the second story, and replacing the roof, this old house became our home and the birthplace of our sister Ruth Ann and brothers David and Lennard. Even though my dad didn't say so, it was a proud moment for him. He had made the grade. For the first time since leaving Irish Creek, Kentucky, he was now a landowner... a person of property!

Another story I remember was the worried look that came over my Dad's face when he first heard the news of the surprise attack on the U.S. Navy in Pearl Harbor by the Japanese on 7 December 1941[11]. The bombing occurred earlier that morning; and because there was no television news available back then, and the time difference, and confusion at Pearl Harbor, the radio broadcast of the event came late Sunday evening in rural Ohio.

Like any six-year old school boy, I went to bed that night confused. Why did the Japanese attack us? We were taught in school to believe that the bad guys were the Germans. The Germans were the ones our British friends feared most, we were told. Would Dad have to help fight the Japanese too?

I knew the sneak attack by the Japanese caught Americans by surprise. We were told later that it was planned by Admiral Yamamoto who had spent some time living in the United States. He knew we had become complacent and that an early Sunday morning attack was an ideal time because many sailors would be off-base on liberty, sleeping late, or getting ready for church services. He knew that no one would be manning their guns, and he felt we would me most vulnerable and would not be expecting an attack. He was right.

It wasn't long after President Franklin Roosevelt's speech before a special session of Congress that many young men, including several of our uncles on both sides of our family, joined or were drafted into the military so they could fight the Japanese and the Germans [11].

This law required that men between the ages of 21 and 35 years of age register with their local Draft Boards. Later, when the U.S. entered WW II, all men aged 18 to 45 were eligible for military service, and all men aged 18 to 36 were required to register. It was not long until men were being drafted into the Army. Men who were married and had children were excluded from the early call-up; so, our Dad was not eligible. Farmers were granted a draft exemption, so my father did not serve in the military. Our uncles on both sides of the family received Uncle Sam's invitation straight away.

As the Allied war machine continued its dramatic buildup, men poured into train and bus stations throughout the United States. Chillicothe's stations were no exception, as our Uncle Jewel and other soon-to-be soldiers, sailors, and marines tugged their luggage, seabags, and duffel bags into the waiting areas to bid farewell to family and friends. Some young men, trying to mask their apprehension, donned brave smiling faces, but most, like our uncles, who were leaving home and the farm for the first time struggled to hold back the fear of their perilous future.

As for me, I remember that several things were rationed during WW II [c]. One had to go to City Hall or the Post Office to get a "Ration Book." It was full of stamps; but, you were only allowed maybe five pounds of sugar each month, depending on how many people were in the family. Gas was rationed too. You could have five gallons for a month if you were a worker. Also, just one tire. Rationing meant that you had to have the stamps to be eligible to buy rationed items.

Gas was one of the first items to be rationed. There were three categories of coupons for civilians. Each automobile had to affix a decal displaying the category in the left corner of the windshield. The colors were black, red, and green. I can't remember which color went with which category. An "A" coupon was available for everyone who owned a car. This allowed the owner to purchase four gallons of gasoline per month. There was a "B" coupon which permitted owners who needed their autos for business to purchase a larger amount--I think it was eight gallons per month. And there were "C" coupons. This allowed a rather unlimited purchase. Our dad had only an "A" coupon.

A national speed limit was imposed at 35 miles per hour. This was the calculated speed which used the least amount of gasoline per mile driven. While this seems like crawling today, the legal top speed before was only 45 mph. Shoes where rationed. I think it was three pairs per year and coupons could be traded among family members. My brothers, sisters, and I usually had one new pair per year as our feet were still growing; but, as I recall our parents and grandparents bought only one new pair of shoes during the entire war. Meat, beef, pork, and lamb, were rationed, but horse meat wasn't. Some families bought it and fed it to their family.

Each fall of the year during the War, we butchered a hog or two and cured the meat by smoking or salting. Our parents decided this was a good idea to guarantee a meat supply and it did not require freezer or meat ration coupons. So, some part of the pig appeared on the table for breakfast, dinner, and supper.

Lard from the butchered hog was used for cooking; the "leaf" lard was kept separate from the ordinary lard. We all enjoyed eating the cracklings that were left over after pressing the lard out of the fat meat. Mom made soap from part of the lard; she cut it into 3 x 4 inch squares and stored it on top of the kitchen cupboard to dry and harden.

I think beef and sugar required different kinds of stamps or tokens. Red tokens made of fiberboard were given as change for meat. Different cuts of meat were charged for different numbers of coupons. Margarine, called "Oleo" back then, was either not rationed or required fewer ration points. Because of the power of national dairy lobby, it was uncolored and came with a little capsule of yellow dye for coloring. One had to let the "Oleo" soften, squeeze the dye onto the margarine and then mix the color in. It took a lot of mixing to make the color spread evenly.

Dad always took sugar and cream in his coffee; but as times got really bad, the first thing he gave up was brown sugar in his coffee. Tobacco was rationed, but he rolled his own. Cigarettes were supplied liberally to the troops. They were always included in the K-rations (now called Meals Ready to Eat) and given out by the Red Cross, Salvation Army, and in USO canteens.

We saved and strained any grease from cooking. It was turned in. I can't remember what it was used for. I think it was somehow used in making bombs. If it was bacon drippings, some of it was kept separate and used for cooking. Mom particularly liked her toast or biscuits dipped in bacon drippings.

Kids learned to make treats by grinding and combining dried fruits rather than making things like fudge or cookies. Those who had older brothers or uncles in the service often received these treats, as they traveled well through the mail. Our mother saved most of her sugar ration to use during canning season.

Families displayed a special small banner in the window if someone from the family was serving in the military. For each son, the flag had one blue star on a white background with a red border. The banner was about 9 inches by 6 inches. If the son died in action the star was gold.

Schools participated in the war effort by having paper drives and milkweed drives two or three times a year. The paper was separated into newspapers and magazines because the slick magazine paper brought a higher price. The milkweed pod was used to make life jackets and parachutes.

Classrooms competed against one other and the class collecting the most paper was treated to a matinee show at the local movie theater. Every school sold Defense Stamps for 10 cents or 25 cents. The stamps went for the purchase of Series E War Bonds which cost $18.75 and would pay $25 after ten years.

Air raid drills were another part of school life. If the school alarm sounded during the day, the students got under their desks for protection. If the school received an advance warning the student was to go home by the most direct route as rapidly as possible, walking, not running, and never stopping to talk to friends along the way.

These drills always seemed to come at the end of the school day. We had to report how long it took us to reach home, and older children were supposed to look out for younger ones they encountered who lived nearby.

Within the small towns, like Tucson, Hallsville, Chillicothe, and Kingston, every block had at least one house with a decal in the window that showed it was a "safe" house--one where a mother was usually home and where any child could seek shelter if caught outside when the bombers came over. Our mother was always home when we'd come from school so we had no sign in our front window, as we lived on a farm.

We also had air raid drills and "blackouts" at home. When the sirens sounded, all lights had to be turned out and windows were covered so that no light shown outside. Street lights would be turned off in town and cars had to stop. The only people allowed outdoors were the air raid wardens. They had flashlights with the lens covered with red cloth or cellophane checking on their neighbors and made sure that enemy bombers would not find their targets by stray lighting. The radio stations announced they were going off the air and to turn one's dial to 640 or 1240 and listen for further instructions.

This directive was to prevent an enemy airplane from honing in on a strong broadcast signal or beam and following the radio signal to the target. Information was broadcast only on the 640 AM and 1240 AM frequencies and you had to switch from station to station. While this system was never used during the war it is still preserved for use during natural disasters. Some people were airplane spotters. They had a badge and an identification card and they had to learn the silhouettes of various planes.

We kept track of the progress of the war through the nightly 15-minute news broadcasts by such icons as Lowell Thomas, Gabriel Heater, or Walter Winchell. Television was not available yet.

Other sources of news were: the newsreels, shown before every main feature at the movies; the weekly magazines, especially *Life, Time, Newsweek;* and, the daily newspapers. We were poor and did not attend the movies too often. While some families tried to protect their children from the bad news of the war, teachers had classroom discussions about it at least once a week. We would locate the places mentioned on a big map of the world hanging on the wall in front of the class.

Civilian automobiles were not made during the war. Automobile plants were immediately converted to making trucks, tanks, and jeeps. Things that had to be imported like rubber and coffee were in very short supply. At that time vegetables were commonly available only in tin cans (not frozen).

Because there was a shortage of copper, pennies were made of steel; and the Mead Paper Mill plant had its electrical wiring made of silver. My Dad said because of the silver the plant had special personnel to guard the wiring.

I remember the day the war ended with Japan in August, 1945. We were not aware that the Japanese had surrendered until we heard it on radio the next day.

Items that most Americans now take for granted were only then obtained with Ration Stamps. Although rationing had ceased on some items at the end of 1945, I can still remember at the age of 10, that sugar and gasoline remained in short supply and rationing did not actually end until the mid-1947.

"Thank goodness for the credit-tab for groceries your Dad had at Billy Boecher's store in Hallsville. If it hadn't been for that, I don't know what we would have done," Mother would say, as we sat around in the evenings in late fall breaking green beans for canning.

I still remember going to Billy's store with Dad even up until just before I went to the Navy. For the six years after WW II, the store didn't change much; except for the big Sinclair Oil sign. Their logo featured the silhouette of a large green dinosaur at all their stations, and they made changes in the logo every few years.

When anyone bought gas at the station (and that was not too often because a lot of people still drove horses and wagons) the kids gathered around the pump to watch how it worked. A store clerk yanked a long handle back and forth, pumping the red-colored gas from an underground storage tank into a huge glass cylinder on top of the pump. A bell rang every time a gallon of gas was released into the car's tank.

Inside the store long wooden shelves extended from the front to the back. On one side the shelves were filled with dry goods, work gloves, women's and children's dresses, men's overalls and shirts, and boxes and boxes of shoes of all sizes for both men and women.

Groceries, chewing tobacco, cigarettes, nails, horseshoes, stovepipe, handsaws and crosscut saws, and other sundry items were kept on the shelves on the other side. In the middle of the store and near the back was a big potbellied wood and coal-burning stove. In front of the stove and arranged in a semicircle were several straight-back, cane-bottom, wood chairs and a few wooden kegs of nails. Seated here on a cold and rainy day one could usually find loafers and a few farmers who would offer at least two new solutions for each of the world's problems daily.

When one of the tobacco chewers needed to spit, he opened the stove door and spitted a brown streak of tobacco juice into the fire, then wiped his mouth on his shirt sleeve or the back of his hand without ever losing his train of thought. Occasionally, when the chewer's aim was off, the tobacco juice would land on the door of the hot stove leaving behind a frying or sizzling sound and a small puff of steam.

A wooden bench about eight-feet long pushed against the back wall provided extra seating for the overflow crowd that would show up during an evening of a special radio broadcast or the blow-by-blow account of a prize fight on Saturday nights. Near the center of the room in the back of the store was a large block of cheese mounted on large chopping block. To protect the cheese from flies, a screen wire covered cage was placed over the block of cheese. A large dirty knife and soda crackers were nearby.

But it was the candy case, filled with hard rock and horehound candy and licorice sticks that we liked best. The fact the candy was behind the glass case and out of reach made us want it even more. The store clerk usually felt sorry for us and would give us each a piece of penny candy during our visits with Dad.

*****

(c) With 2016 being the 75th year since Pearl Harbor and with the reaction to the event all but dwindled from memory, books and articles continue to appear. The traditional interpretations of the facts prevail; but, conspiracy theorists have found a new forum to promote their blame and doubts on the Internet.

"What is the chief end of man? --to get
rich. In what way? --dishonestly if we can;
honestly if we must."

----Mark Twain-1871.

CHAPTER 4

Hopewell Saga & Reunions

*O*ur Grandfather Elijah was not Herodotus, but he was a born story-teller. Through and through. If today, he told his stories on Twitter or Facebook they would go viral with a million hits a day. He learned how from his father Leander and his grandfather James before him.

Sitting around the fireplace or campfire, walking or driving down country roads through the wooded hills, he would tell stories at the drop of a hat. We usually asked for Indian stories. He said sometimes, with a little wink, that he may have a little Shawnee blood in him and "I'd be gosh-darn proud if I did."

Our family made visits to Mound City State Park just outside Chillicothe. Here the Mound-Builders called the Hopewell [12] people built more than two dozen burial mounds and surrounded them with a low earthen wall around two thousand years before. Today, the 120-acre site is being considered for nomination to the UNESCO World Heritage List [12].

"Chillicothe was not Ohio's first capital," Grandfather Elijah would say. "Mound City" was. "They knew about the world around them herbal medicines, bone to make a fish hook; and nearby a potter mixes water and clay to make bowls and jars. "And you guys would probably starve if you didn't have fast-food."

Then he would start one of his many stories.

"The Hopewell [d,12] cremated their dead in what we call a charnel house. They placed all kinds of stuff around the dead: copper figures, arrowheads, shells, and pipes. And the important people got fancy things, really beautiful works of art that you can see in museums. Then they all got together and brought hundreds and hundreds of handwoven baskets full of dirt and built these mounds we see. "I'd like to see you guys do that!"

"Now, stop for a moment, allow your mind to drift backwards and imagine a mid-summer afternoon in a small village just over yonder. Just think if you could build a house like the Hopewell, using sticks and twigs for walls, covering them with mud and clay, and then putting on a thatched roof made with straw or water reeds. Try it sometime. I bet you would be having fun spearing fish along the Scioto River flowing right down the hill, but not really fun because if you didn't catch anything you didn't have supper. And women and small children are picking blackberries near the woods.

"In the center of the village a toolmaker is chipping flint arrows and bird-points, the flint probably came from Flint Ridge, near Newark just north of here, and the black shiny obsidian came all the way from the Rockies. Maybe someone is drilling a hole in a large mussel shell to make a hoe or taking a piece of bone to make a fishhook; and, nearby a potter mixes water and clay to make bowls and jars. And you guys would probably starve if you didn't have fast-food."

"They knew what plants worked for each illness. Many of the drugs used today the Hopewell used: quinine, ephedrine, Novocain, ipecac, witch-hazel, just to name a few."

"Pyramids were being built in Egypt around 2000 BCE, marble temples were constructed in Greece around 600 BCE, and these Hopewell mounds in Chillicothe 1000-600 BCE. This is old, old sacred ground we're standin' on, folks. And we're eatin' hot dogs. Ain't that somethin'?"

The Elijah and Pearlie Jane Adams family reunion was held every year on the first Sunday in August at the Logan Elm State Park, a few miles west of Kingston. At each reunion after the blessing my grandfather, Elijah, who stood more than 6 feet and 5 inches tall would stand near the trunk of the giant Elm and tell the story of Chief Logan. As a young lad, I didn't fully appreciate the sight of a 'giant' Grandfather Elijah being overshadowed by what was one of the largest, grandest, and historic trees in the country.

"Now listen up," he would begin, "I know you heard this story last year, but it is a good story. No. It is a great story. And I'll keep telling it as long as I have even one listener.

"In the spring of 1774 Chief Logan of the Mingo tribe and his family and friends were invited to a party by a group of Virginia trappers. These lousy good-for-nothin' trappers were not the ideal of the frontier. Logan was unable to attend, but he told his family to go and have a good time. He never saw them again.

"The trappers let the whiskey run freely, and when the Mingos were off guard the trappers killed them all, women and children, and strung the insides of Logan's pregnant sister along the banks of the Scioto River. War continued until autumn. The two sides eventually met near Chillicothe to determine peace terms [e]. Chief Logan was invited to the conference, but refused to attend. He played his hunches. He did, however, deliver a speech to a few men under a huge Elm tree north of present day Chillicothe. It is called 'Logan's Lament' and is, perhaps, the finest speech ever given on the frontier:

'I appeal to any white man to say if he ever entered Logan's cabin hungry and I gave him not meat; if ever he came cold or naked and I gave him not meat; if ever he came cold or naked and I gave him not clothing ... Col. Cresap, the last spring, in cold blood and unprovoked, murdered all the relatives of Logan, not sparing even my women and children. There runs not a drop of my blood in the veins of any living creature ... Who is there to mourn for Logan? Not one'.

"That speech was the talk of the frontier. It moved the whites as much as the Indians. Many soldiers memorized the

lines (I think they read like somethin'
from the Bible) and talked about them
around the campfire. One militiaman
would greet another with, 'Who is there to
mourn for Logan?" And another would
reply, 'No one!'

My Dad told me later that the tree
had fallen to Elm blight, its great branches
weakened by storms and high winds.
Logan's Elm was cut down to prevent
injury to park visitors. Now there is a
plaque and only us to mourn for "Logan."

(d). More information may be obtained at the
Hopewell Culture National Historical Park,
Chillicothe, Ohio 45601.

---

[e] It has been said by many that nowhere on the
American frontier was the clash of cultures more
violent than on the Ohio frontier. First settled by
migrating Indians of the Iroquois Confederacy about
the 1700s and later by white settlers, Ohio became
the crucible which set Indian and Virginia military
policy throughout the region. There, Shawnees,
Wyandots, Mingos, and Delawares, among others,
fought to preserve their land claims. A land of
opportunity, refuge, and violence for both Indians
and whites, Ohio served as the political, economic,
and social foundations for the settlement of the Old
Northwest Territory.

Here is another one of Grandfather Elijah's stories. And it's a good one.

"Now listen up. I'm going to tell you a story about a woman who was so fantastic you probably won't believe a word I say. Would you believe a woman who stood six and one-half feet tall and went into battle buck-naked and painted her body blue? A woman who spoke four languages and served as peacemaker and interpreter for the Shawnee, the settlers, and the British; and, practiced the work of a shaman to heal people. One heckuva woman, I'd say. No wonder her Shawnee name, Nonhelema, translates as 'not-a-man.' The British nicknamed her 'Grenadier Squaw' because of her stature they said. But I think it is because they were afraid of her.

"She was born around 1772 on Scippo Creek not far from here. When she was about 40 years old she had a spiritual vision. She saw that war between her people, Great Britain, and the growing number of American settlers would never end. She became known as the Peace Chief, and although her people continued to fight, Nonhelema 'studied war no more.'"

Absent from my grandfather's declarations during the 1950's and 60's was an explanation of more important history in an area just a little north of Logan Elm called "Pickaway Plains." Today it is a wide area of rich farmland sprinkled with houses neatly placed between the rolling hills starting about three miles south of present day Circleville, Ohio, and extending several miles to the north. During the time of inhabitation by the Shawnee the area was covered by prairie vegetation and mostly grasses.

Shawnee, founded at least three villages in this area [f]. The first village was called "Cornstalk Town" which was located on the north bank of the Scippo Creek just east of the present-day U.S. Highway 23 and approximately where Gold Cliff State Park is today. The town was named for the principal Chief Cornstalk who gave battle at Point Pleasant against the British on 10 October 1774, which may have been the "Shot that was heard around the World" not the ones fired six months later at Lexington and Concord.

"Grenadier Squaw Village," Grandpa would continue saying," was located opposite the Scippo Creek from Cornstalk Town on Ohio Route 48 or Emerson Road. The town was named for Cornstalk's sister Nonhelema, whom the British called the "Grenadier Squaw." In spite of the slaughter of her family by Lord Dunmore's militia, headed by Colonel Andrew Lewis and Colonel Thomas Cresap, the founding father from the dark side in American Colonial history, she remained loyal to the British land-grabbers.

"In 1796 at Fort Pitt, General Benjamin Logan captured Nonhelema and her Shawnee husband, Moluntha. He was executed. Nonhelema, tired and her health broken, died. She was honored by President Thomas Jefferson, Daniel Boone, and General George Rogers Clark.

"So, everybody, what have we learned? The women's movement is nothing new. It started right here in Pickaway County more than two hundred years previous. I think Nonhelema would be proud of us."

{f} Today, any thought given or plaque raised as a marker to this earlier Indian habitation is overshadowed by the bumper crops of corn and soybeans taken each year from that hallowed ground. The Treaty of Camp Charlotte, near present day Circleville, was negotiated with the Ohio Valley Indians after the Battle of Point Pleasant in 1774, ending Lord Dunmore's War. The Ohio River became the boundary between the Indians and whites, and the Shawnees agreed to stop attacking travelers on the river. The treaty secured peace for Ohio, Kentucky, and Virginia settlers, which lasted through the early part of the American Revolution.

"We teach our children that the ground beneath their feet is the ashes of their grandfathers."

--Chief Seattle

*****

CHAPTER 5

Health Care

During the Depression, Dad worked on the farm and there were no health insurance benefits for the family. This was before childhood immunizations, and the transmission of communicable and infectious diseases was not well understood.

We did not have yearly health check-ups and, since we were all born at home, we were not taken to a doctor unless we were critically ill. The only physician nearby was Doctor Hemmeger. He was born in the river town of Marietta, Ohio, on 10 September 1874, 86 years after the first settlement in the Northwest Territory. He graduated from the Starling Medical College in Columbus, Ohio in 1895, and "hung out his shingle" in Laurelville before moving to the nearby town of Adelphi a year later.

My first memory of the doctor was when I was about five-years-old and he came to the house and told our parents that we had German measles and the family would have to be quarantined. A bright red and embarrassing sign representing an infectious disease warning dangled on our front door for more than two weeks.

Immunizations were not available then, so we got viral childhood diseases including: whooping-cough, mumps, and chickenpox. I remember the stigma of

39

having that Public Health Quarantine sign hanging on our door for years to come.

When we became ill our parents relied upon self-diagnosis and treatment with folk remedies [13,14]. Having allergies to animal dander or ragweed pollen and getting desensitized with low-doses of allergen, as an example, would have been a luxury that we could not afford. (My first visit to a dentist was when I joined the U.S. Navy).

As I remember, our family used home preparations of sugar-tit, sassafras tea, drops of coal oil placed onto a tablespoon of sugar, turpentine, pork, and onion poultice. I can still recall the terrible taste of kerosene on the sugar...the sweetness didn't help the medicine go down. These measures were often supplemented with commercial concoctions like Vick's Salve, Troutman's Cough Syrup, Cloverine Salve, Milk of Magnesia, Carter's Liver Pills, and the J.R. Watkins Company's line of products.

For cuts, bumps, and bruises tincture of iodine or Mercurochrome were the first things pulled from the medicine cabinet for use. I can still recall my Dad saying: "put the red stuff on it." We all dreaded hearing those words because the sting of the "red stuff" was usually greater than the pain from the wound

The use of herbal and home remedies in health care was commonplace in Kentucky, southeastern Ohio, and other parts of Appalachia. It was routinely practiced in the 18th and 19th centuries, and remained in use by my parents to some degree into the late 1950's.

I was told by my Grandmother that the common Mullein was used widely as a folk medicine when she was growing up in Kentucky. She said that many of her relatives and others used the leaves to make a medicinal tea for treatment of lung complaints. I remember seeing the plant in Kentucky and on the farm in southeastern Ohio. Its tall stout stems are covered with woolly, oblong leaves during the first year of growth; and yellow blooms follow on the spike around the middle of the second summer.

Dad said it was known in Europe as the "Velvet Plant," and it was probably brought here by the early settlers. I also read that the Romans used the dried stalk as a funeral torch and the Greeks used its dried leaves for lamp wicks. The plant is still abundant in the meadows and along country roads, and its tall stalks are a common site in the summer landscape.

My friend, Ron, calls it "Lamb's Wool." When he took his Scout troop on nature hikes he always pointed out the unexpected softness of the ordinary looking weed. The Scouts would "ooh" and "aah." Ron wanted to describe the feel as "sensuous." But he was afraid that a Scout might ask him what the word meant.

My grandmother also told me that the reason for the use of such herbal medicines was the great distances to a physician's office. Back then it was nearly a day's journey by car to the nearest doctor and the roads twisted and turned and were extremely rough. During the winter months, they became holes of mud and mire and frozen deep ruts. Many roads in Johnson County were former wagon trails. In some places the gravel creek beds became the road, and during high water they were treacherous. These bad road conditions fostered a dependence on folk medicine and home cures.

She also told me that she remembers when doctors used leeches for some medical problems and came to the home and did bloodletting for other maladies. She said that long before the use of aspirin and the development of the stethoscope, it was not uncommon to find doctors making house calls with a box of leeches and sharp knives in their medical kits.

Some may say we have made progress in medical care since my grandmother was growing up in the late 1800's. Nevertheless, many similar products with questionable benefit are still being offered on late-night television, advertised in throw-away magazines, as popup adds in social media platforms, and frequently presented in sub-liminal messages as part of authentic public health announcements. They have been purported to be beneficial in some diseases to: "aid digestion", "improve heart health", "boost brain function", and to offer some resolution to men with "erectile dysfunction." **(See Addendum A below)**.

*****

CHAPTER 6
Gods, Goddesses, & Myths

If I remember correctly, in the King James Version of the Bible (1 Corinthians 13:11) it is written: "When I was a child, I spoke as a child, I understood as a child, I thought as a child; but when I became a man, I put away childish things." For me, when I was young, I was taught to believe, and I truly wanted to believe, in the literal teachings from the Bible; but, as I grew older, something was missing. The words and events were unsubstantiated, void of logic, unproven, and one "must have faith" was always a prerequisite [15].

Now, I appreciate the several explanations for the meaning of those metaphorical contemporary statements from the Bible by ministers and priests. However, at an early age one does not understand the meanings of such magical and mystical thinking which is most dominant at this time in their lives. During this age, children strongly believe that their personal thoughts or actions have a direct effect on what happens in the rest of the world. Therefore, if they experience some tragedy, such as a death in the family or even a pet, they do not understand and their minds create a reason to feel directly responsible.

Some developmental psychologists have stated a child's thinking may be dominated by perceptions of physical features, meaning that if they are told that a family member or a pet has gone away then the child will have difficulty comprehending the transformation of the loved one or the pet not being around anymore. Magical thinking is evident here since the child may believe that the family member or pet being gone is just temporary. Their young minds at this stage do not understand the finality of death, and magical thinking bridges the gap.

Children who use magical thinking not only feel that they are responsible for an event or events occurring, they feel they are capable of reversing an event simply by thinking about it and wishing for a change or to explain the unexplainable. If they are given an explanation of death as being God's will or the person and or pet has gone to a better place, children may become very angry at death, God, or adults in general. Or they may be angry at themselves, and somehow feel responsible for the death. If a child's ideas about an event are incorrect because of their magical thinking, there is a possibility that the conclusions the child makes could result in long-term beliefs and behavior's that create difficulty for the child as they mature [15].

Now, what are we taught to believe regarding the Christian Bible? We were repeatedly exposed to the teachings of the preachers in the Poes Run Baptist Church or from Sunday school as taught in the two Methodist churches nearby. We were exposed to the "Wrath of Hell" early in our young lives while attending Etam Church or Walnut Valley Church on Walnut Creek Road.

We were threatened by the so-called vengeance of God because of our wicked ways, and yet on the other hand by going to church week after week and hearing a mixed message of what an evangelical minister had organized as his evidence of God's goodness, or omniscience, or whatever, we could be forgiven for our sins. Yet, during revivals and camp meetings their preaching was intended to awaken a religious fervor in all who attended!

Their sermons were not unlike the themes of evangelist Billy Sunday, a baseball player and one of the most celebrated evangelists, (1862-1935) who always gave his followers a large dose of hellfire and damnation. Invariability, he would sort through recent events, biblical parables, moments in his life, or things that people had told him, and paint a picture that somewhat gelled for the few moments before other events that didn't quite fit into the picture at all had a chance to occur to you.

Finally, after an extended diatribe he would admit---even relish in the possibility that everything didn't add up--- that any reality regarding faith was incomprehensible; that the failure of our understanding was the greatest proof of all ... not out of goodness or omniscience, but the power of God and our lack of faith was at fault...there again, that word called "faith" again and again...a word that was frequently used but was difficult for anyone to give real meaning ...that intangible thing without form or vision.

As he spoke of power of God and faith, his voice deepened, his gestures widened and they became more exaggerated and animated, his eyes would light up, and tears would flow down his face. These spectacular scenes were not unlike those from other scandals played out years on television by other evangelical televangelists such as Jimmy Swaggart, Jim, and Tammy Bakker, before they were accused of infidelity or caught with their hands in the cookie jar. They even had the gull to challenge anyone for questioning the power of God and lacking faith.

I frequently became frightened in church as a young lad who had said a few dirty swear words and had told a fib or two earlier during the week. For sure, the preacher's message made me feel that if I didn't change my ways I was surely "going to burn in Hell!" Near the end of the service, I would again promise Jesus that I would not do all those "bad things" during the next week.

My recollections of questioning the power of Jesus or God and feeling disappointed with the lack of personal help from "Him" occurred early and most vividly in my life on at least three occasions: the first time was while attending my maternal grandmother's funeral in 1944. While standing near my mother during the viewing, I noticed tears flowing down her cheeks. Innocently, I looked up and whispered: "Don't cry Mom, if He can raise Lazarus, He will do the same for Grandma!" (I never did learn from the Bible the exact time when Jesus became God).

Four months later, that same feeling of disappointment was present during my Grandfather's funeral, and the third occasion, which left me with a complete sense of total disillusionment, was at my cousin, Irene Castle's funeral. I could not understand why an "all knowing" and "loving God" would allow a young and innocent child to become ill and die? To me at that age, Jesus or God was being a monster!

Surely, He would perform one of His miracles in this situation too? After all we were taught in Sunday school that He not only brought Lazarus back to life, but He repeatedly performed this grand act on other occasions (John 11:1-45), and another time when Jesus also raised Jairus's daughter from the dead (Matthew 9:18-26; Mark 5:21-43; Luke 8:52-56); and, a Widow's Son (Luke 8:40-56).

Little did I know that such allegorical claims that were presented or interpreted as fact in biblical history and gained traction with such alarming ease, was spreading both errors to outright fundamental misconceptions? (As Richard Dawkins once stated: "Do not indoctrinate your children. Teach them how to think for themselves, and how to disagree with you)."

The "laying on of hands" to cure a person of an illness or disease that was promoted to be an alleged power begged science and logic; but, many of the evangelical ministers still practice it during their "Events" today.

Surprised? Shocked? Little did we naive farm boys know that the sexual eccentricities, as depicted in Tennessee Williams' passion-filled essays, plays, or movies, such as "Street Car Named Desire" and "Cat on a Hot Tin Roof" were taboo topics although they were shown at drive-in movies. Throughout the 1950's, censors seized every opportunity to abbreviate, abrogate, or expunge screen sequences they deemed too sexy for American audiences---who continued to cling to their puritanical beliefs, myths, and hang-ups about sex. Those self-righteous guardians of our pseudo-Victorian morality were omnipresent then as well as today within the church of the evangelical "Christian Right."

Besides being down right frightened as a child watching such exorcism-like activities, it wasn't until much later after I joined the Navy and assisted the Navy Chaplain who provided religious services on Sunday mornings that I became more enlightened as to religious pluralism. My help consisted only of pushing the portable alter from ward to ward in a Naval Hospital in order for the sick could receive the Word.

It was at this period in my life that I began to really question the attitude or policy regarding the diversity in religion, and it was here I had the resources available to research some of the scientific literature for any evidence of anyone having such "healing" powers and abilities to cure the ill---including those imminent and eminent powers of a Catholic Priest! [6].

48

"Those who make you believe absurdities can make you commit atrocities."

Subsequently, during military service with the Marines and alongside chaplains in the field, I acquired a greater appreciation of their duties in providing comfort to injured servicemen and women who are daunted by the misgivings of killing in war and harbor the uncertainties of any sanction of their actions by God. Providing counsel and memorial services are unique duties that the chaplains are required to provide, regardless of the setting.

Later, during the Vietnam era in the 1960's, most chaplains were Christian, from nearly all denominations; and, more recently in Iraq and Afghanistan more than a few dozen were from other faiths, including Jews and Muslims. Even though they spent more time tending their own flock, leading services and tending to dietary restrictions, the Muslims chaplains were often called on to explain the tenets of their faith to all our military. The top brass wants to know about the theology and the mind-set of the troops while serving in the Arab countries. But most of their time is spent ministering to troops and providing comfort to those of all faiths.

I remember that Memorial Day or "Decoration Day," as most members of my family called it, was an important time in our early lives. School was out for the summer, and it meant we would travel to Kentucky and visit with our Aunts, Uncles, and cousins on both sides of the families.

Along with the fun and games, it was a more serious time too.

That was time when we would visit grave sites, attend all-day church services, and have lunch and dinner on the ground, but the military significance of Decoration Day was not lost and forgotten to our family. It was to honor those who had given their lives in Service to our great country. My own genealogy research of our family tree [6, 7] revealed numerous relatives who fought and died for our country; in the Civil War, World War I and World War II.

As a small boy, I listened intently to the stories from my uncles and I wanted to know all about the military, where they had served, and the things they had seen and done. Back then I didn't realize or appreciate why they didn't want to say much about their combat experiences, and they sometimes got that far look in their eyes, shook their head, and instead elected to talk only about a couple old buddies.

They sometimes would mention long ago boot camps, bivouacs, long marches and sore feet; but they smiled the most when they recalled liberties and furloughs on foreign shores and in distant cities in faraway countries with buddies and friends whom they got to know better than family members they had known for years.

Although I was only a child during World War II, I still remember seeing pictures in *Life* and *Look* magazines of American flag-draped coffins being off loaded from railroad cars at the depot and being released to their families. The families and communities were devastated. I specifically remember the solemn look on the faces of the Soldiers, Marines and Sailors in their full dress blue uniforms when they escorted their fallen brothers' home.

So many times, over the following years I have stood at graves of friends, like Budd Lang, and family members, including Ted Cannon and Lennard Campbell, who have served our country in the military. I have seen the veterans from the American Legion and the Veterans of Foreign Wars on Grave Detail gather around, fire their volleys to honor the fallen, and give the final salute to their fellow comrades.

I have looked around at the people in mourning who openly wept. And I have felt terribly saddened when the bagpiper played "Amazing Grace," when the bugler played "Taps," after that first shovel of dirt landed atop the lowered casket, and the flag was lowered to half-mast. This scene has been played out all too frequently within my own family at military funerals; my wife's parents were both buried in Arlington National Cemetery with full honors.

Fortunately, both friends and family who have served in the military and have returned home have assimilated into public life without calling attention to themselves. They are the Quiet Ones. The one thing I tell my grandchildren is that heroism is a much higher attainment than anything that occurs in sports. To be a hero requires taking risk and exposing yourself to jeopardy. Heroism requires nobility of purpose, action that is beyond your own self-interest. Not from design or a plan, it just happens and it may require the ultimate sacrifice. Why do they do this, you ask?

It is because as John F. Kennedy said: "We shall pay any price, bear any burden, meet any hardship, support any friend, oppose any foe, in order to assure the survival and the success of liberty."

The American military has always been made up of ordinary men and women. In combat or in emergencies, ordinary people do extraordinary things. If they come home, you will not see those burning or disgracing the flag, wearing only parts of a uniform, rushing out to buy a Humvee, or purchasing an AK-47 for "target practice." They are the Quiet Ones!

I have been left to ponder the philosophical words of Christopher Hitchens: "If it wasn't for death, there would be no need for religion."

*****

CHAPTER 7

Readin', Writin', and Chiggers

𝔚hen school began each year at Harrison Elementary School, near Mooresville, we devoted our time to our studies. By today's standards, Harrison School would have been condemned and closed. One reason: there were only four classrooms inside the brick building and each room housed two grades of students; first and second grades were in the same room; third and fourth grades were together, etc. One teacher was assigned to each room, and while the teacher was teaching students in one grade, the other grade was in study hall.

Two other small rooms in the building included a lunch room (a place to eat our peanut butter and jelly sandwiches we brought from home). A second room was the Principal's office. There was no cafeteria to serve hot food, nor vending machine with cold drinks. The toilets were located at some distance down a long path in back of the school.

Life experiences of growing up in a small school such as Harrison produces good and bad memories. These also include life -long friends. However, it was in this school that I remember a coming of age event that caused a loss of innocence and considerable embarrassment.

It occurred on a Monday morning in study hall, following a Sunday afternoon of fishing along Walnut Creek in late

September. While sitting on the grass along the creek bank, I had become infested with chiggers—those little red critters!

Summer wasn't only sunburn, heat, and humidity, it was chiggers. Chigger bites first showed up as annoying red bumps. Then the itch began. The affected area would become hard with red welts developing near the surface. From your feet and ankles upward (and especially at those private places your mother told you not to scratch in public).

Savage scratching continued; every welt became a persistent, exquisitely itching preoccupation that continued to irritate for days and even weeks. Many believe they are some type of bug. Folklore tells us that they burrow under our skin and die, that they drink our blood, and that they can be killed by suffocation with nail polish or by bathing with bleach, alcohol, turpentine, or even salt water. Surprisingly, all those popular remedies are just plain wrong.

Chiggers are not bugs, or any other type of insect. Chiggers are the larval form of a specific family of mites. Mites are arachnids, like spiders and scorpions, and are closely related to ticks. These mites are unique among the many mite families in that only the larval stage feeds on vertebrate animals; chiggers dine on us only in their early stage of life, and later become vegetarians that live in the soil.

In my case, about twenty-four hours after the initial chigger bites to my groin area and lower legs, red and raised lesions appeared. The agony of chigger bites was only relieved by scratching. I could scratch only by placing my hand inside my bib overalls.

To the girl who was seated two rows to my left, it must have appeared that I "playing with myself". It wasn't long thereafter, during a next class break that she approached our teacher, Mr. Brown, to report what she had imagined me doing. Within minutes Mr. Brown took me into his office and proceeded to call my dad. He instructed my dad to come to the school and take me home for the remainder of the day.

In the meantime, Mr. Brown made no comment directly to me, nor asked for an explanation. Had there been a school nurse available in the schools back then, this misunderstanding could have quickly resolved. Mr. Brown assumed the adolescent girl's comments were true. It goes without elaborating that his dilemma caused a terrible embarrassment to my dad and me. On our way home, he said nothing about the girl's claim, and I was too embarrassed to mention it.

My life-long friend included William "Bill" Garnes. He was a few years older than I and one of the most fascinating individuals I have ever met. We attended Harrison School and were from rural backgrounds. Bill was unique in that he possessed an aura of a young Abe Lincoln. His house was on a hill-side farm located at the end of Spud Run Road, near

Tucson, Ohio. His parents owned a couple of horses and a milk cow and Bill raised several goats. He claimed goats were easy to care for and they did a good job of clearing away the underbrush near his house.

Bill had a reputation of a bookworm in elementary school. When we transferred to high school in Adelphi, Ohio, I really got to know and appreciate his intellect. His appearance by this time was that of a gangly teenager who always wore tennis shoes that were two sizes too large. And he had a different stride to his walk, long, extended steps and, as he neared his desk, just about fall into his seat.

His trademark was the very short pencils that he brought to class. They were two or three long and they all looked as if they were sharpened with a pocketknife. When he got an audience, he was as confident discussing Will Durant, Charles Darwin, or Rene Descartes, as he was being one of Principle Ed Weston's "Select Six" who made up the advanced math class at Adelphi High.

As for Bill, he was always reading something, even encyclopedias. When he finished his class studies, he would grab another edition of the encyclopedia and read it cover to cover. He could quote most of it verbatim on the school bus. Many thought him to be eccentric, but to the Adams boys, he was our friend—just Plain Bill.

Bill had a great fascination with the stars—not only the ones in skirts—but the celestial ones, as well. He was fascinated with the whole universe, the cosmos, and the stars. Occasionally, we would lie on the ground staring into the heavens during the summer months and he would name all the stars in the vast galaxy. Who has not gazed with wonder at the night sky, especially from in a dark site far away from the city lights? This great canopy of stars stretching overhead suggests that our world is part of a vastly larger cosmos.

Bill introduced me to words like Osiris, Horus, and Ra. He tried to explain to me the whole of Egyptian and Greek religions as they related to their many gods, with precise reference to the solar god, who was considered the supreme symbol or metaphor for God. These new lessons were too complex for me as someone who had only heard the stories of Jesus as the Son of God in Sunday School.

Bill excelled in Algebra, Geometry, Trigonometry, and Physics. I was satisfied just to learn Business Math from my favorite teacher, Ms. Mary Ann Cryder.

Brother Ed once asked her what he had to do to get an "A" in her Math class. She replied that he would have to give her the red, flannel shirt he was wearing that day. Sometime later, she told me that leaving her classes that evening, she found Ed's red shirt hanging on the antenna of her car.

She was considered a good friend of our family. Her parents, Earl and Ada Cryder, were teachers too. They also owned a large farm where our dad and grandfather, Elijah, had once worked as farmhands.

CHAPTER 8

The Adams Farm

In 1950, when I was a freshman in high school some property nearby came up for sale. After convincing Mom, it was a good buy, my parents agreed that they should take out a loan and purchase the land.

This became known as the Adams' Farm. The Farm was a rough and tumble 145 acres of rolling hills and dense underbrush. On certain cloudy nights in the hills near Rattlesnake Knob you could hardly see your hand in front of your face. It was like walking through a cave. But what mysteries those caves held for our imaginations - our own Adventureland.

There were no buildings on the land, so Dad bought a sawmill, and we cut the timber to produce the lumber to build a barn and a farmhouse. Dad was as tough as a winter apple. He continued to work eight-hour days at Mead Paper Mill while Bert, Ed and I dug a full-size basement using only a horse-drawn scoop, shovel and mattock. We laid the cement block for foundation, and sawed the lumber for construction. After two-years of labor, and with Dad's help on the weekends, we moved into our new homestead.

Bert, Ed, and I are the oldest of eight children and we worked long hours with our parents to clear the underbrush, plant seeds, work the garden, and the farm to provide food for our table and grain and hay to feed the livestock.

We planted: Irish and sweet potatoes, sweet corn and field corn, peas, tomatoes, cabbage, lettuce, onions, peppers, rhubarb, several kinds of beans, watermelons, and cantaloupes. Many pints and quarts of good, chemical-free foodstuffs were canned or pickled. We dug pits, lined them with straw and buried potatoes and cabbages to preserve through the winter. Cabbage was preserved in salt-brine to make sauerkraut.

Our mother often said, "You may like potatoes and not be Irish, but you can't be Irish and not like potatoes."

Potatoes kept us and a lot of other folks from starvation. None of us one could remember when there weren't potatoes. We fried everything in lard and we could have your taters "soft fried" or fried golden brown in a skillet sitting on a wood-burning stove. Today, nutritionists would protest vigorously at the idea of such a fat-filled diet.

Our younger brothers and sisters were too small to provide much help with manual labor, so they were assigned easier chores and did themselves proud. Bernard Ray picked blackberries and raspberries and helped Mom make jams and jellies. (Brother Lenard was not yet born).

When the berries became "dead ripe" (when they are ready to fall off the vines), all of us jumped in to help. On berry-picking mornings we rose before sunrise. We dressed in old overalls, long-sleeved shirts, and long socks and gumboots. To reduce chigger attacks, we tied binder twine around our ankles. Milk pails, gallon buckets, coffee cans, and wicker baskets were used to collect the juicy berries.

A few trees on the hillside provided needed shade for us in heavy clothing, and we were always on the lookout for snakes, sweat bees, and chiggers. Old Jack, a black and white mongrel, held bragging rights for killing snakes. Copperheads and rattlesnakes were commonplace in those hills. As our best friend and protector, he always escorted us to the berry patch, scouting for snakes. Old Jack would quickly grab a snake near its middle section after it would strike at him, and he would shake it from left to right so hard and fast the snake's head would snap off. One or two times I remember, a copperhead bit Old Jack's on his hind leg. He would just lie around, very sick, not eating and licking his swollen leg, but he always got better.

Our sister, Elizabeth Jane, or Betty Jane as we called her, helped Mom with supper, cooking and cleaning up. We had a wood-burning stove for cooking, and another one to heat the house. Keeping the stoves supplied with firewood was a monumental task. We used an ax and crosscut saw, and everyone pitched in.

Betty Jane also helped Mom with the washing and ironing. They used a "flat-iron" that was heated on the cook stove. Our clothing had to be ironed.

In those days, a sewing machine was a necessity and Mom had a Singer treadle machine. In the middle of the afternoon Mom was usually in her and Dad's bedroom sewing stitches and singing hymns. This is where we learned the words to our old favorite hymns like "Precious Memories" and "Amazing Grace."

All our clothes were washed by hand using lye-soap in water heated in a large wash-tub over an open, wood fire in the back yard. Later, in 1950, Dad bought Mom a gasoline motor-powered wringer washing machine. She was the proudest woman on Walnut Creek.

Mom and Dad were strict disciplinarians. We were taught to obey them. We knew, all too well, the consequences of disobedience; a thrashing from Dad's leather belt to "tan our hides." Nevertheless, we knew our parents loved us, and we were taught to respect them.

At the time, I didn't appreciate the many lessons I learned from Dad. I can still picture my dad in early spring as he plowed a plot for our family garden or prepared the hillside fields for planting corn. I see the old team of horses and hear his commands of "Gee!" and "Haw!" He worked hard as he wrestled with the reins, keeping the breaking plow upright and straight.

His shirt would be soaked with sweat, which cooled him from the rays of sun and made his hard slog a little easier. More pleasing was the Mason jar of ice-cold well-water that I'd bring him as a small boy. I would head out across the field to deliver my special treat to Dad. I loved to feel the warm spring earth as I walked bare-foot down the freshly tilled rows. With the soil sifting between my toes, I felt as if I was walking on bed of feathers.

I would quietly follow behind Dad to the end of the row and wait until he turned the team around and noticed me; then, I'd hold up the Mason jar of cold water and present it to him as if it were the greatest offering of his life. As he drank, the icy water trickled down his chin onto his stained work shirt and bib overalls and cooled him all over. On one occasion, he extended his hand for a healthy shake and said, "Thank you, God knows I needed that."

He believed in hard work, and taught us the importance of good morals and integrity. A firm hand-shake was the seal of one's word. There were no ifs, ands, or buts with Dad; everything was as up-front and straight-forward as the long furrows he plowed. He was from the old school where people know when you are sick and care when you die.

Nevertheless, as kids growing up, we invariably found ourselves with a bit of leisure time to kill - just enough time to get into trouble. It wasn't hard to find ways to get into mischief, especially during the "dog days of summer" when the corn was laid-by and the garden crops were not ready for harvest. There were few things we enjoyed more than playing practical jokes on each other.

There is the story of Bert (who was our leader when it came to stunts and tricks) and the Old Peddler, Bill Butts (his real name!) He had converted an old red school bus into a country store on wheels. His route took him from Jackson, Ohio, across the back roads of Ross County, and eventually to our neck of the woods by mid-afternoon every Thursday. Before stopping at our house, he would pull over along Hough Road and eat lunch under the shade of maple trees.

After lunch, he would break out some of his magazines with pictures of nude and scantily-clad women to view. Before moving on, he would throw away the old magazines into the ditch. Later, we would retrieve the magazines for our afternoon viewing pleasure. Once, Bert gathered a couple of the discarded magazines and stuck them in the back pockets of his bib-overalls.

Mr. Butts carried an array of sundry items on the old bus and Mom bought some of her household items from him. There was chicken feed, coal oil, canned goods, "light" bread, cookies, pots and pans, all sorts of dry goods; and, also Rawleigh products and Cloverine Salve for medical purposes. She also bought some of her spices, herbal items, flavoring extracts, liniments, and other patent medicines and household products.

After Bert made the purchases for Mom, he carried the bags of groceries back to the house. He placed the bags on the kitchen table and he turned around to go back outside. Then Mom saw the magazines and grabbed one of them from his back pocket.

All hell broke loose.

"What are you doing looking at pictures of these nasty and dirty old women? "Where did you get this trash anyway? "Wait 'til I tell your Dad. He will deal with you when he gets home young man!"

We knew what that meant: a trip to the "woodshed" for Bert.

Come the end of September, we each knew what had to be done to prepare for the long, snowy, cold, winter months in southeastern Ohio; so, before daybreak we were always up and ready to go. After breakfast, we were off to the barn to feed the livestock, milk the cows, and get ready for school. After school, we changed clothes and soon be on the way to the cornfield to cut the corn and place it into shocks that stood upright in the field.

By early November, we would shuck the corn that was later taken to the feed-mill for grinding into feed for the livestock. And, there was always the need to cut more wood for future use in the wood-burning stoves.

Christmas on the farm was the time when all the children looked forward to going to the woods, selecting the right tree, cutting it, dragging it back, bringing it into the house, and decorating it for the holidays. For us, in the late 1940's and early 1950's, there were no lights or brightly colored balls placed on the tree. We cut paper of various colors into narrow strips, glued them together with a mixture of corn starch, flour, and water, and made a paper chain links that was wrapped around the tree. Sometime, we used popcorn on a string and wrapped them around the tree.

We were small children and still believed in Santa, on Christmas Eve we would each attach our name to one of Dad's long, clean, work socks; hang it near the tree; and off to bed we would go, wishing for that special present to magically be there the next morning. Lo and behold, sure enough, there to welcome us was an apple, an orange or a tangerine, and a couple pieces rock-hard or horehound candy neatly packed into the toe of the sock.

Occasionally, if we had been exceptionally good during the year, we would also find a neatly wrapped package containing a new pair of bib-overalls or a flannel shirt. There were no toys, such as Hot-Wheels, roller-skates or bikes to be found on Christmas morning. Being poor, and like most families of the time, we were told to be grateful for our health, and we all looked forward to Mom's Christmas dinner.

Despite various hardships and many inconveniences by today's standards, we were blessed with freedom; and the support of a strong and caring family.

*****

CHAPTER 9

Village Smithy & Mathematician

Mr. Charles "Charlie" W. Brown was the Principle of Harrison School during seven of my eight years of elementary education. He taught the seventh-and eighth-grade students. In general math class, he frequently incorporated word puzzles as homework for the seventh-grade students. On one occasion, he told our class that the puzzle included a farmer who had purchased nineteen apple trees to plant for an orchard. The farmer instructed his hired-hand to plant the 19 trees in 9 straight rows with 5 trees in each row.

The assignment was to draw on paper what the orchard would look like diagrammatically. We were told that we had two days to work on the problem. After struggling the first night without success, my Dad suggested that I take the problem to our old friend and local blacksmith, Nelson Kerns. I always looked forward to any excuse to visit his blacksmith shop.

Good or bad, rich or poor, big farmers or small, they were all his customers. They congregated at his blacksmith shop on rainy or clear days, at all hours of the day and for various reasons. While the old gray mare was being shod or a wagon wheel was being fixed, there was time for talk, argument, gossip, ridicule, and political debate. A lot of horse trading was conducted by the glow of the old forges.

For my brothers and me, the blacksmith shop held a special attraction. To us, the shop was a place of mystery and excitement, full of good sounds and unique smells.

The poem, "The Village Blacksmith" by Henry Wadsworth Longfellow (1807–1882), presents an image of a blacksmith of giant proportions; brawny enough to pick up a horse off the ground single-handedly or have bend a piece of cold iron into a wagon wheel rim with his bare hands.

As I look back over the past eighty years of my life, I vividly remember our daily visits to his blacksmith shop located near the top of the hill on Hough road. He didn't stand under the spreading chestnut tree; in fact, as a young boy I admired the way he could get around as well as he did with one leg shorter than the other. I often wondered why he a physical impairment, but never had the courage to ask why. He was still a giant of a man to me.

Mr. Kerns lived alone is a modest house near the blacksmith shop. His shop was inside a weather-beaten, clapboard building without any paint that had been expanded over time to include three sections built on the slope of the hill. Behind the shop was his famous potato patch; in addition to using the produce for food, he used potatoes to trade for goods and services. Bartering was still a means of survival back in those days. He traded potatoes with a local widow lady, Mrs. Barnes, who did his laundry each week.

He was a familiar figure in his long-split leather apron. His hands were usually black from handling iron rods and bars and hammers of various sizes and shapes. His long iron tongs, handmade from his own forge, had many uses and were made in many shapes. No blacksmith shop was complete without them. Here was the "flat bit", "crooked bit", hammer, hoop, and round and square tongs. Everything had their specific uses and he knew how to use them.

There were two forges equipped with bellows. The coals in them were heated by forced air from the bellows that were worked by a long pole overhead in an up and down motion. These bellows forced air up in a tube to the bottom of the grating; thus, the iron surrounded by coal and coke could be heated white-hot. In the second forge, he used a hand crank that generated the air. Into each forge from time to time he inserted his iron bars and rods to be heated. He could tell when the iron was at the exact temperature at which the metals should be pounded on his anvil. The iron was held by his long tongs in one hand and the hammer in the other. Hot sparks would fly in every direction like thousands of lighting bugs at night when he hit the hot iron with his hammer.

He allowed the rod to heat to a cherry red color, and when the iron was shaped into the desired design with a hammer, he dropped the hot metal into a half- barrel made of wood containing water that was always kept nearby. This added the proper temper to the iron.

If he wanted to make a wagon wheel rim he would run his hot iron rod through a series of rollers which were turned by hand. The result was a perfect circle. The ends were then placed into the hot coals until each end was at the exact heat. Years of experience had taught him this little secret. The large circle was then lifted to the anvil with tongs and the ends were pounded thus making a seal or bond into a solid metal ring.

My brothers and I visited the shop to watch this old man perform his wonders. The floor of the shop was dirt and very black. There were no wooden floors. The ground was literally covered with hundreds of nuts, ends of bolts, used horseshoe nails, and pieces of small iron bars ground into the soil. The sides of the building had hundreds of iron rods of all sizes. The large iron anvil, resting on a large wooden block, had its familiar ring. Near the anvil were countless tools, all stacked on end or hanging on the block so that each special item was within reach when needed.

Hammers of many varieties and anvils of different shapes and numerous chisels were found in his shop. One chisel that fitted into the anvil slot was called a "hardy". He had his favorite pincers, used to shoe horses. Other types were used for nails and bolts.

One type of anvil had small holes in each corner. These holes were rectangular and tapered for the purpose of making nails. He made his own horseshoe nails, and all sorts of strange looking nails, which were used in wood flooring. He made large and ornamental hinges used for cabin and barn doors.

When he had a supply of iron, he made sled runners, scythes, hoes, corn cutters, and numerous varieties of hooks so much in great demand by the farmers back then. In fact, there was hardly any farm implement or utensil that he could not make.

There was an old, dust-covered, 1934 Chevy Roadster with a rumble seat in back. In front of the old car was an area where the farmer brought his horse to be fitted for new shoes. The horseshoe sizes ran from number three to twelve, if I remember correctly. They were made for draft horses or work horses and they were usually hanging on pegs fastened to the large wood studding and each size was marked on the shoe. On the side of two wood posts was a ring through which the strap to the horse's halter or bridal was inserted and then pulled tight to hold the horse in the shoeing process. (Years later, Brother Ed told me he was permitted to drive the old Roadster one time before the old blacksmith died).

Like every blacksmith, he had his long tool box. In it were his horse-shoe nails, a special hammer for driving the nails into the hoof, his rasp, and a dozen other tools he found necessary to use.

Near the wall was the hand operated drill press, used to drill holes in the tire iron as well as in farm equipment which farmers brought for repair. On a long bench was his large vise. This tool had a long iron leg that ran into the ground. This gave added support to the bench and the vise when a large object had to be held securely. On this bench laid numerous odd shaped hammers, punches and other mysterious objects which had specific purposes around the shop I am sure.

As I grew older, I looked at the diverse role of our blacksmith. Not only was he the local toolmaker and "engineer" he played all kinds of roles: teacher, dentist, doctor, undertaker, veterinary surgeon, and horse dealer or trader. He helped me with some math problems from time to time, and he also held an important office as Squire in the community. He was the choice for all these positions as his job demanded a certain level of intellect, numeric skills, and old-fashioned business sense.

Regarding the math problem, he not only solved the problem as expected, but introduced a supplementary solution as well. As for me personally, he was my mentor and our friend.

*****

CHAPTER 10

The Blizzard of 1950

Severe snowstorms have occurred in Ohio during the winter months. The Thanksgiving snowstorm of 1950 was one of the earliest and deepest in Ohio's history. The entire state had more than 10 inches of snow, and many communities in the eastern half of Ohio, including Chillicothe, measured 20 to 30 inches of snow.

As the storm strengthened, winds increased to more than 40 mph and a severe cold wave swept the state early on Friday the 24th of November dropping temperatures to near zero. The worst part came the next day; blizzard conditions blanketed Ohio. By late evening, snow drifts were more than 25 feet deep.

The storm continued through Sunday and by Monday morning snow depths reached 33 inches on the old farm. Bulldozers were used in Chillicothe to clear the streets and side roads so that ambulances could reach those who were ill or in need of food, but they didn't reach the rural areas where we lived. Ohio Gov. Frank Lausche declared a state of emergency and the Ohio National Guard used Jeeps to transport people to hospitals and deliver food to rural homes. Utility wires and trees were blown down by winds as high as 60 mph. Many buildings collapsed under the weight of the snow. On the farm one end of the tin roof on the corncrib was pulled up by the wind.

Despite the snow and high winds, the annual football game between the University of Michigan and The Ohio State University- the classic rivalry- went on as scheduled in Columbus. The game became to be known as the "Blizzard Bowl."

On Saturday morning frost glazed the kitchen windows, the wind was blowing the snow around, and the temperature was near zero. We appreciated the warm house after feeding the farm animals. Then mother told us that she was nearly out of flour, cornmeal, and other foodstuffs. She didn't think we could get out until the roads were cleared, and then maybe someone could get to the store for provisions.

Travel by vehicle was impossible because the county workers had not cleared the roads. We were snow bound. But we were not alone. The Price and the Skaggs families, our nearby neighbors, were also unable to go to the store because of the heavy and deep snow.

On Monday Gordon Price, Bert, and I saddled-up our horses and traveled five miles to Billy Boucher's store (Fig. #2) in Hallsville on horseback and purchased the needed supplies. We set out about noon, while a light snow was still falling, with the plan of returning home by dark.

Our travel along the gravel road was slow for the first few miles as the horses strained to make their way through the heavy drifts. Progress became more difficult as the snowfall became heaver and the wind stronger. We struggled.

By this time, we could barely see the dim lights glowing from a few houses in the distant town of Hallsville; the temperature had dropped to below freezing; snow had accumulated another three or four inches on top of the six to seven-feet snow drifts; and our travel on horseback became even more treacherous and difficult for the horses during these last hours of daylight.

We decided to leave the horses because they were worn out and sore and could develop muscle cramps. We tied their reins to a fence and began the walk across the fields through the snow to the town. At first glance, the snowdrifts in the field appeared less deep than along the road.

Staggering along the ditch, we fought the bitter cold and blowing snow. I lost much of the feeling in my fingers. The holes in my old worn, brown Jersey gloves and my thin Levi jacket provided little warmth and protection. Even so, we grabbed the empty feed sacks that were tied around the saddle horns, and set out across the frozen, snow-covered field.

We headed towards Route 180, hoping it would have been plowed because it was a State highway. We were right. Sure, enough, the snow had been cleared and we made it to Billy Boucher's store before it closed, and ordered our provisions.

After explaining our situation of having to walk back to the horses, Mr. Boucher gave each of us a new pair of brown Jersey gloves and wished us well. We ventured back into the freezing weather with feed sacks of our groceries slung over our shoulders.

The snow had stopped by the time we reached the horses. The moon was shining through a partially overcast sky and the temperature had dropped a few more degrees. We were almost back to the horses, then I stepped in a rut, turned my ankle, and fell into a snowdrift.

I struggled to get up. I regained my footing and limped onward while listening to Bert and Gordon make fun of me. We tied the open ends of our two sacks together and tossed them across the back of our horse like a sling, and climbed aboard.

The ride back home seemed less difficult for the horses as we avoided some of the larger drifts of snow under a moonlit-sky. However, my sprained ankle throbbed with pain as we slowly moved onward in the cold, late night air.

We arrived home after midnight, fed the horses, helped put away our foodstuff, and told our parents about our adventures. Mom heated a pan of hot water on the cook-stove, and I soaked my foot to ease the pain and reduce the swelling. We warmed ourselves in front of a roaring fire in the old wood-stove and went to bed.

The snow melted too rapidly during those first few days of December. Walnut Creek was out of its banks, the Scioto River was well over flood stage as far south as Portsmouth, and the Ohio River caused flooding downriver in Cincinnati.

Ol' Man Winter wasn't finished with us. It was a long cold winter. One snowstorm after another blanketed the landscape. Snowdrifts had to be cleared before we could reach the barn to do morning chores. The watering trough that normally held water for the cows was frozen over with four or five inches of ice every evening, and the old cook-stove and the old potbellied stove that heated the house gobbled up great piles of wood and coal.

No matter how cozy the farmhouse, there were times when one simply had to venture out the door. Thankfully, there were ways to avoid a shivery but necessary trip to the little house out back with its icy seat and drafty door. Chamber pots postponed the excursion for a while, and sometimes evoked a smile to lighten the long and dreary day.

As summer prepared for winter, so winter's chores presaged the coming of summer. Old tools were repaired and new ones made.

******

CHAPTER 11

Boys will be Boys & Chickens or Eggs

Bert tried to be funny one evening when Ed and I were in the barn milking the cows. After we finished, Bert challenged us to a footrace back to the house. It was almost dark outside and all we could make out were shadowy images. We had to aim for the light coming from the windows in the house about 200 yards from the barn and follow the dirt path and go through the gap in the barbed wire fence. The gap was a passageway in and out of the corral created by taking down a section of the fence. There we could easily walk over the barbwire.

While Ed and I were doing the milking, Bert re-attached the barbed wire and closed the gap. Bert and I started to race. I was in the lead. And just before reaching what I thought was the gap, Bert dropped out of the race and I ran head-long into the barbed wire. I received several deep cuts across my face, chest, and legs and had one helluva time trying to explain the cuts to Mom. I have yet to get even with Bert on that one!

There is another event involving Bert where facts have recently been revealed and the identity of the real culprit has become known. It was during the latter part of November 1952, and we had a light snowfall overnight – a "Dominque snow" as Mom called it, where you can see intermittent parts of the ground.

There was just enough snow so Bert could track a rabbit back to its hole in the base of an old oak tree in the woods on the back part of the farm. He was unable to get to the rabbit, so he decided to try one of the old tricks he had heard about. He was going to build a fire and smoke it out.

After an hour, Bert still wasn't getting the results he had hoped for and it was late afternoon and getting dark and Dad was supposed to take us to basketball practice that evening. Bert was not one to give up easily. He gathered some more leaves and stuffed them back into the hole and tried again to light a match to the leaves. The leaves were still too wet from the snow so they would not catch fire. However, the enormous amount of smoke produced was what Bert wanted and needed to "smoke out the rabbit."

Hurrying, so as not to be late, he placed a rock over the hole so the rabbit could not get out, and then rushed back to the house to get ready to go to practice.

About an hour into practice, the school janitor got a call from our neighbor, Howard Miller, who said our woods were on fire in the back part of the farm. Bert and I jumped into the car with Dad and we took off racing back the 12-miles to the farm; followed closely behind were Freddy Barton, Larry Good, Glenn Congrove and other members of the ball team. About three miles from the farm, Freddy's car slid off the road into a ditch on Walnut Creek.

Arriving at the scene of the accident, the other drivers stopped their cars to aid

Freddy and his passengers. No one was injured, but they were late to the fire. In the meantime, our neighbors, including Howard Miller and his two sons, Verne Coey and three of his sons, and our brother Ed had the fire pretty much under control when Bert, Dad and I arrived at the scene. The next two hours were spent raking back leaves, cutting underbrush, shoveling soil over the burnt area and securing a burn line.

The brushfire out, we had to hook up old Dolly and Prince and pull Freddie's car out of the ditch. Fortunately, the damage to his car was limited to a loss of paint to the right side.

Mom blamed Verne Coey with starting the fire, because he was always coon hunting back on that part of the farm. At that time, no one knew that the fire had been started by someone who wanted to smoke out a rabbit.

During my young years at home, the kitchen was the best-smelling room in the old farmhouse when Mom was fixing breakfast. The best times were the winter months when snow covered the ground and the temperature outside hovered near zero. We children slept upstairs, three boys to a bed, and I wouldn't let my feet touch the chilly, wood floor until I could smell coffee brewing.

Often, I would hear her rattling the pots and pans or cast iron skillets in preparation of breakfast. That great taste of eggs, pork chops, biscuits and gravy that were fried or baked in the same old iron skillets after frying the bacon in sausage grease remains in my memory.

Mom's cast iron skillets served extra duty after breakfast. She used one of them again every night to bake cornbread from scratch. She used it again on Sundays to fry apples, potatoes, and the best brown-and-crisp chicken I have ever eaten.

Also, when I was growing up poultry-raising was a haphazard endeavor based a little on science and a lot on chance and folklore. Mom had only three breeds of chickens in her flock, white Leghorn, Dominique, and Plymouth Rock. The Leghorn laid large, white eggs practically every day. (In winter, she used petroleum jelly on the comb to prevent frostbite).

The Dominique breed, with a black and white barred plumage that was hawk-colored, and she felt this served in making the bird less conspicuous to predators. They did well in hot and humid climates and have close feathering that not only protected the birds in cold weather, but provided material for the pillows and featherbeds, these birds are first and foremost egg producers with small- to medium-sized brown eggs.

The Plymouth Rock looked like the Dominique breed and was considered a dual-purpose breed, raised both for its meat and for its brown eggs. It was more resistant to cold, easy to manage, and a good sitter.

Because Bantams are famously broody, Mom did keep an occasional Bantam hen around to use to hatch eggs from other hens, but their eggs were too small; to complement their yolks, she claimed you'll need more whites than most angel food cake recipes called for.

Mom raised her chickens range free. She felt confinement prevented a happy, healthy flock. Some people advised against mixing ages, but she never had trouble with older birds picking on younger ones.

Mom believed the recommendations contained in the Old Farmer's Almanac when it came to weather forecasts, planting charts, astronomical data, and articles on a number of other topics including how to raise chickens. Some of her beliefs may have simply been from old wives' tales?

Nevertheless, when Mom had a broody hen or "settin' hen" in the flock, she would candle the eggs and she placed only fertile eggs in the nest to be hatched on the new phase of the moon. For added assurance with her 'Lucky Mojo," she placed a rusty nail in the nest to protect the eggs and the hen from weasels, skunks, and blacksnakes that often-raided hen houses. I worked every time.

*****

CHAPTER 12

Good Times and Bad Girls.

During my junior year of high school at Adelphi, I attempted to play basketball, but I was never that good. I was considered the sixth man on the varsity team. The coach penalized me for not making all the practices during the week because of farm chores.

We had a good cheer leading squad, but our cheerleaders were not fancy or gymnastic as they are today. They were energetic, dedicated, and possessed good lungs. They were loyal and strongly supported their team—win or lose.

The standout cheerleader was Alice Beemer and she was Freddie Barton's girlfriend. He was the star player, and it stood to reason that the star would date the best-looking cheerleader. That did not prevent me from having a crush on her; and, after all we were good friends.

There was disagreement among the cheerleaders about the type of uniform to wear. Most families were not rich and the school had a limited budget, so selecting a uniform was a difficult task. Would the skirts be pleated or plain? Would the sweaters be turtleneck or regular? Would their shoes be low-topped, high-topped, or black-and-white oxfords? These were major decisions, and heated disputes were frequent.

The sweaters were very bulky and they had a thick letter "A" for Adelphi on the front. Most of the girl's bodies appeared less "physically mature" than today's youth, and the letter would loosely cover the entire front. Selecting matching colors was sometimes a problem, and the washing detergents in the early 1950's were not as safe as today's products. At the beginning of the year all sweaters were the same color- white. And, after two washings the colors were varied, and the shapes were baggier.

The skirts were plain, long, flowing Spanish styles, and they hung midway between the knee and the ankle. Bobbie socks were worn and the tops were turned down just above the ankle. When the cheerleaders spun around during a routine on the gym floor, their long skirts followed them like a bullfighter's cape.

The cheers were not as dramatic as they are today. They were sort of standard and simple at all the schools in the district. Each game would begin with the cheerleading squads from both teams meeting and forming a circle in the middle of the floor joining hands and doing a unity cheer of friendship. Unless an untoward event occurred due to a slip or fall, not as much as a knee cap or thigh were ever in view. The only extravagant routine where a bottom was momentarily exposed may have occurred during a cartwheel. This not seeing "anything" caused the cheerleader's body to remain a mystery to all the ball players.

Adelphia High School closed its doors at the end of the 1952 School Year and because of consolidation of the school district, my last year was at Southeastern High School located in the small town of Richmondale, Ohio. The year was going by rapidly and most of the seniors were making tentative plans regarding their uncertain future.

For most Southeastern High School students, except those who had lost a relative or a friend in the fighting, the "Korean Conflict," [20,21] seemed so remote and distant. Our study of world history, current events, and the daily news accounts of the "War" did little to formulate a real understanding or appreciation of terms like: "the 38th parallel that divided North and South Korea, Old Baldy, Bunker Hill, White Horse Mountain, Triangle Hill, Sniper Ridge, Pork Chop Hill, Heartbreak Ridge were just terms that had no real relationship in our daily lives [20,21]. We were just students; innocent, protected, and immune to the evils of the real world.

Most high school seniors were preoccupied with last-minute fund-raising projects needed to help offset the cost of the Senior Trip to Washington, D.C. For a few students in our "Class of 1953," the week-long stay in D.C. would represent our first travel out of state, and for most of us, our first extended time away from home.

For many, the travel to Washington represented a "rite of passage" into the real world. As youth, being protected and coddled for years, we would drink in deep delight of liberty, utter its wild, barbaric bellow, and we soon would advance to conquer and remold the world.

From time to time during the remainder of the last school year, jokes and humor were commonplace in the classroom. In every class-room there is usually a Peck's bad boy. Peck was a fictional star in newspaper stories created by George W. Peck in the late 1800's. Peck was a naughty or mischievous lad who loved to play sneaky pranks on others for the sheer pleasure of creating mayhem. Our class was no exception. We had two of Peck's bad boys: Fred Montgomery and Richard Collette.

Do you remember the old desks where the seats were attached to the desk from behind and the seats would fold down and there would be a crack in the fold of the seat? Norma (Sis) Cunningham had sneaked her brother's shirt out that morning and wore it to school. It was one of those shirts with a long tail. We were in Mrs. Higby's Literature class and Sis was sitting in front of Fred who decided he was going to give Sis a hot seat. He didn't realize her shirt tail was hanging through the crack in her seat, and he set her shirt tail ablaze with his cigarette lighter. Suddenly, realizing what had just occurred, Sis jumped out of her seat and, out of concern for her wellbeing, both Fred and Richard started beating her on the rear end.

At the time, Mrs. Higby had her back to the class, writing on the chalkboard, and by the time she turned around, everybody was back in their seats acting studious. She asks, "Does anyone smell smoke?"

To this day, she never knew what happened. Some said she was much too old and slow on the uptake to teach, but she hung in there. Of course, we loved her because we could get by with almost anything in her class. And, we all pitched in to buy Sis's brother a new shirt. Sis and Fred both had many laughs about this event later.

As for me, I always looked forward to the many discussions we had in Ms. Bauer's Psychology class regarding Nurture vs. Nature. One was the famous "Scopes Monkey Trial" in Tennessee that occurred years back. One day I would take the pro-creation position and the next day I would argue in favor of the evolution theory. Regardless of which side of the debate I was on, I felt that each side had good points and it was difficult to conclude whether Nature was at fault or if things observed were influenced by one's environment.

Some serious discussions did occur between students and our faculty advisors regarding our futures. Some were going to get married, raise a family, and spend their lives working at Mead Paper Company. A few of the guys were going to take over the family farm. We were all required to register at our local Draft Board, and chances were good that we would have to serve in the military.

College was at the top of a short list for six or seven of the 43 students. For me, the expense of college was beyond my economic means. Maybe later, after a tour of duty in the Navy, I would return home and go to college.

For a few of the guys like Jim Detillion, Melvin Thacker, and Jim Skaggs, post-graduation would be a difficult transition from being a star on the high school football team or basketball team one year to dealing with daily life after graduation.

Some may say they were called the "Fabulous Fifties" for a reason. Holy Moley, Shazam...gee whiz, golly, you and who's army? What a decade!" The big war, WWII, was over, business was booming, and "...What, me worry?" Many, including my brothers who were too young to be drafted, remained care-free. They knew Uncle Sam and John Wayne would take care of the war, while on the home front Ike and Willie Mays would lead us on to victory.

Compared to today, the economy was solid during the 1950's. The cost of a gallon of gas was 20 cents and the average cost of a new car was $1,650. Jobs were plentiful and mad money seemed to be available for every fad and fashion that swept the country. Hoola hoops, Frisbees, coon-skin caps kept the kids occupied. The adults got caught up in bomb shelters, Bermuda shorts, pink button-down shirts, pegged pants, sack dresses, pop-off beads, poodle haircuts, the gospel according to

Dr. Kinsey, Dr. Seuss, and also the launch of the Sputnik satellite by the Russians.

"From Here to Eternity" and "Shane" were the hit movies in 1953. The number one pastime was watching T.V. in its infant stages. Westerns, variety shows, and situation comedies were the main fare. Among them were "Maverick," "Gunsmoke," "Sid Caesar," "Sgt. Bilko," and shows with family-fun couples with whom most everyone could identify "Ozzie and Harriett," "Burns and Allen," "Lucy and Desi," and "Honeymooners", the battling Ralph and Alice Cramden.

For the more sophisticated, there were "The Dinah Shore Show" and "The Loretta Young Show." Even though they were not educational programs, they were better than the trash-like reality shows offered today.

In the 1950's, I discovered Marilyn Monroe in her infamous dress, or in a state of undress for her calendar pictures. According to our preacher at the time, if we were to view her motion pictures, we would be exposed to mortal sin and we would surely go to hell. From my first glimpse, I forgot all about mortal sin and going to hell. The heat was on and Marilyn played a large part in my later fantasies. I even had her picture inside my locker aboard ship.

At the dawn of the fifties, as far as our soiled innocence was concerned, we knew zilch about making out. We were told that there were good girls and there were bad girls. Good girls never smoked or stayed out after 10 p.m. They wore loose sweaters, straight skirts, pony tails, and they all wanted to be nurses, secretaries, or Grace Kelly when they grew up.

Bad girls were all fast, and they wore short-shorts or skin-tight pedal pushers. They peroxided their hair, wore gobs of eye makeup, carried false ID's in their wallets, and read "Peyton Place" so many times that they could quote every line verbatim. They always hung around with "hoods" who wore their hair in greasy duck-tails, wore leather jackets, carried a church key on their belts, and wore Levi jeans that showed the outline of a condom they had in their hip pocket. This type of guy would spout lines from Mickey Spillane or some other off-color character, bad-assed their elders, and always bragged about their ability to "score" on the first date.

My dad said repeatedly: "All these guys needed to straighten them out was a nice girl and a hitch in the Army." What we all needed was a little time, a little time to grow up!

Without a doubt, some of the most beautiful songs by such notables as Frank Sinatra, Tony Bennett, and Patti Page, just to name a few, came out in the early fifties.

Looking back over those years now, not unlike the setting and characters in the movie entitled "The Last Picture Show." Some of the events in our lives as new graduates paralleled those in the film.

We were young, impression-able, and our hormone levels had peaked. In fact, once could replace Anarene, Texas depicted in the film with Chillicothe, Ohio, in the early 1950's, and little would have changed—a main drag, a Sohio station instead of a Texaco station, a café, a feed store, old pickup trucks, farm lands all around, and a pool hall where youngsters with a restless yearning to grow up drank beer out of brown bottles. They giggled and elbowed each other in the ribs followed by the telling of off-color jokes, while the older boys played pool and told tales of would-be affairs during bygone days.

In a much wider context the movie was really about larger transitions: from youth to adulthood for the young people, from a frustrated and bored middle age to an even less promising future for the older folks, and from a town with some social cohesiveness to a town dealing with the isolating effects of a questionable future economy and the advent of television. Yet, there we were living out the same lives of frustration with our own unrealized dreams in our own generation. Or, throughout our own lives since graduation, it was all there: the comedy, tragedy, romance, desperation, treachery, love, death, infidelity, ennui, and abandonment—it was all there.

Unknown to me at that time, I had adopted what I later learned was somewhat like the Yin-Yang Eastern philosophy of life; for every negative, there is a positive reaction! My negative was that I did not have the financial resources to go to college, so I joined the U.S. Navy. Any positive reaction would have to come later in my life.

*****

CHAPTER 13

Leaving for the Navy

Little was said by my Father or me during that early morning 12-mile drive from the old farm on Walnut Creek Road to the Grey-hound Bus Station in Chillicothe, Ohio.

"Do you have your tickets and all your stuff," he asked again for the third time since breakfast. I repeated as the old 1948 Dodge came to a halt at the stop sign on corners of Charleston Pike and Walnut Creek Road.

It had rained for two days and it was still coming down like "cats and dogs." The drops were falling so fast the wiper blades labored to keep the windshield clear to see the gravel road ahead. I searched for my freshly ironed and neatly folded handkerchief my mother had given me and wiped the moisture from the windshield on the driver's side.

"All the leaves will be off the trees after this rain," I murmured as I turned away and wiped my eyes before putting the wet handkerchief back into the Levi jacket I was wearing.

"Yeah," Dad replied.

Nothing more was said during the rest of the trip. Nothing else could be said. The oldest of his six sons was leaving for the U.S. Navy.

There was little traffic on the streets in town and all the businesses were closed on Main Street—except the Bus Station.

"We're early," I said.

"You don't want to miss your bus to Columbus, Son," he said, as he pulled my old, worn, and dilapidated suitcase from the back seat of the car.

"I know, but we have 45 minutes to wait before the bus leaves."

"You'd better check-in so you can get a good seat," he insisted, as he pulled a pack of Camels from his shirt pocket. Being early was not new for him. He always arrived at least 30 minutes early before clocking-in at Mead Paper Mill where he had worked for several years.

We waited motionless and silent for several minutes on one of the wooden benches in the middle of the station as I watched a stray cat eat a piece of discarded sandwich in one corner of the dirty waiting room.

"You want a cup of coffee?" I asked, breaking the silence. "We still have a few minutes before the bus is due."

"Yeah, do you need some more money for your trip?"

"No," I answered. "Mom gave me twenty dollars this morning. Besides, the Navy Recruiter said I would not need any money because the Navy would pay for the tickets and everything, you know."

The coffee must have been brewed the night before because it was too strong to drink, even after adding more milk. That didn't matter, the station-keeper had announced the on-time arrival of the bus from Wheeling, West Virginia, and we knew it would soon be loading.

I raked the change from the counter and walked over to the newsstand to buy a copy of the *Chillicothe Gazette* to read on the bus.

"Here, let me carry your bag to the bus," Dad said as we slowly walked towards the doorway. Make sure you write your Mom when you are all settled in and everything. You know how she worries about you boys."

"Yes, maybe I'll even have a chance to call her."

The driver took my bag and I turned to face Dad. Before I could say anything, he placed his hand on my shoulder and said, "Take care of yourself and be careful, Son. You know the war is still going on over there."

I didn't bother reminding him that an armistice agreement was signed almost three months earlier on 27 July 1953, ending the Korean War [20, 21]. I could see in his eyes that this was a difficult moment for him. I just turned away and climbed aboard the bus.

As the bus crossed the C & O railroad tracks, I remembered that Chillicothe once served as the capital of the Northwest Territory. I was also reminded that the constitutional convention made Chillicothe the state's first capital in 1803; and, Thomas Worthington the sixth governor of Ohio moved the seat of state government from Chillicothe to Columbus in 1816 [22].

I often marveled at the fact that just a mile or so west of Chillicothe, on a beautiful elevation commanding a magnificent easterly-view of the fertile valley along the meandering Scioto River and its bounding Mount Logan hills, is Adena. This former home of Governor Worthington is a stone mansion erected in 1806, was then one the most elegant homes west of the Appalachian Mountains. Today, the building and grounds, embosomed in shrubbery, and near a beautiful flower garden, are eloquently maintained by the State of Ohio [21].

Before Worthington became governor, Chillicothe and the area nearby presented a somewhat different picture. Most of the early settlers in the south-central and southeastern part of the state were farmers and small business people who came through Cumberland Gap in eastern Kentucky and eventually up the Ohio River into southeastern Ohio. They were of English, Irish, and Scotch descent, call "Scot-Irish" [5]. Some of the surnames included Adams, Cory, Igou, McDougal, Hare, McLandburg, Graham, Candlish, Ross, Dun, Carlisle, McCoy, McAdou, McConnell, Kerr, Wright, Griffis, Day, Kendrich, and Gillfillian.

The few roads in Ohio at this time were muddy trails; and when the spring thaw and the rains came most of these became impassable. Getting products to market was difficult for these pioneer farmers. Farmers living near the Scioto River and Salt Creek built rafts or flatboats and floated their farm produce, grain, salt-cured pork, and booze down the river to market in Portsmouth, and down the Ohio and Mississippi Rivers to national and foreign markets in New Orleans.

Few farmers could afford the time and risk of taking their own cargo overland on such rugged, dangerous, and long journey (that frequently proved to be unprofitable). It was not until the state capital moved from Chillicothe to Columbus in 1816 that any serious consideration was given to solving this economic and commercial problem. Most of the solutions came from outside the state.

Investors in New York had the foresight of building a canal connecting New York City and the Hudson River (a distance of 363 miles) to Lake Erie at Buffalo for commercial interest of providing a direct route for products produced in the Mid-West. The powers-to be in Ohio took positive steps to build the Canal running north and south across the state in an effort to link the state's commerce to the eastern markets [23].

By 1832 the Ohio and Erie Canal was busy with commercial traffic and Chillicothe benefited greatly with the numerous small business, start-ups of heavy industry, expansion of farming, and the provision for transporting of agricultural products to new markets down river and to the east via the canal. The Canal produced rapid growth in Chillicothe and helped make the town a staging area for the westward migration of eager and adventurous pioneers [23].

There were a few white settlers in the Northwest Territory and by 1860 more than one in five Americans lived in the Northwest Territory. The geographic center of the population of the United States was near Chillicothe, Ohio [22, 23]. To accommodate the increased numbers of new workers and the transit influx of western travelers into Chillicothe, several hotels were built. These hotels were soon targeted by conservative groups who felt they would become watering holes best known for hauntings, prostitution rings, smugglers' dens, and mafia activity.

Along with the legal dance halls and taverns that hosted theatrical plays or musical concerts there were claims of illicit activities. To satisfy the demand for booze from the clientele in the taverns, two of the town's most prominent residents, Thomas Worthington and Duncan McArthur (Ohio's sixth and eleventh governors), operated distilleries nearby.

By mid-1800s there were more than 52 saloons in Chillicothe. To the church goers and members of the fledging "Tea Totaling-Do-Gooders Society" within the Temperance Movement, the numerous taverns on Water Street that ran along flanking the canal represented the "shady-side" of town.

Any amorous, effeminate words, lascivious, or lust-exciting dancing, be it on the stage, in the many bars, or even in the ally-ways along Water Street was considered by the "Do-gooders" a dangerous incendiary of lust; an ordinary occasion of lewdness, and a preparative to much whoredom, adultery, and wantonness action that was surely becoming common place, if not stopped, was certainly a giant leap towards hell and damnation of all the citizenry in Chillicothe.

Although such entertainment naturally follows progress in any city, the prostitution was not widespread. There was the occasional notorious Houses of Harlotry or Houses of Ill Repute that sprang up in Chillicothe. Many of the Soiled Doves had rooms in the hotels along Water and High Streets and from Mulberry up to Walnut Street. Even in the 1950's, as a high school student, the mere mention of Water Street conjured up some intended or presumed thoughts that excited some lascivious adolescent feelings.

These trivial facts did little to alleviate my feeling of sadness as the bus roared onward in the morning darkness.

Of interest is the fact that with growing competition from railroads and highways, and the opening of the St. Lawrence Seaway in 1959, commercial traffic on the old Canal System declined dramatically in the latter part of the 20th century [23].

CHAPTER 14

In the Navy Now

The sun rose over the nearby Mount Logan Hills during the two-hour ride to Columbus. The rain had stopped and I spent the remainder of the trip looking out the window without speaking to anyone because I was deep in thought about leaving family and friends. This was going to be the first time being on my own and away from home for a long time. This was really something new for a boy from the farm, but I still felt a strong sense of pride. I was proud and eager to join the Navy!

At the bus station in Columbus, I was met by two men in Navy uniforms. "Come with us," one said. "We are still looking for two other guys who are supposed to be here also," the second one added. Moments later, the other young men arrived. We all climbed into a dark-blue van with a sign on the doors that read: "U.S. Navy" and "Official Use Only." Within minutes we arrived at the Naval Receiving Station and were processed into the U.S. Navy on the 6 October 1953.

Reveille came early the next morning to the yelling of the Sentry on Duty. Later in the afternoon, all the new Navy recruits who were bound for Bainbridge, Maryland, were *"mustered"* and instructed to load a bus for a ride to the train station. There were eight men and one woman who boarded the train for what became our long, overnight journey to Bainbridge.

The train departed the station in Columbus at 5 o'clock for the long 15-hour ride to Washington, D.C., and then on to Havre de' Grac, Maryland.

Most of the guys spent the early evening in the Club Car drinking and telling stories about their reasons for joining the Service. I had learned the names of four of the men, and they talked about going to boot camp together and maybe later serving on the same ship together.

A couple of guys even knew what they wanted to do in the Navy. One guy said he joined to avoid being arrested. Another said he was leaving because of a breakup with his girlfriend. A third fellow said he had joined the Naval Reserves in high school, and active duty was now part of his obligation.

As for me, I didn't have the slightest idea what I would be doing but, I was sure interested in attending one of the several schools that was being offered by the Navy. After my second drink, I found little in common with most of the men who were by now getting a bit drunk and a little too loud with their conversation.

I returned to the sleeping car to do some reading. The sun had set and faint lights could now be seen in the windows of houses near the railroad tracks as the train raced through the early evening. Even the overhead light in the railroad car did little to overcome the darkness. Moments later, the conductor came through the car and announced; "Next stop Charleston. Charleston, West Virginia".

In Charleston, I noticed that two women came aboard the train; one lady was traveling with two small children. The second woman, as best I could tell through the dirty window of the train, was an attractively dressed, young lady who was carrying a suitcase, and traveling alone. As she climbed aboard the car ahead, I also noticed that she had exceptionally long, red hair that caught my eyes.

I wonder where she is going, I thought as she climbed aboard.

As the train pulled out of the station, I converted my small cabin into a sleeping berth. An hour went by when I heard the voices of two people nearby. The first was that of the conductor who said, "This is your sleeping berth, number 4B.

"What time does the dining car open in the morning?" A female voice inquired.

"Six-o'clock, Madam," was his reply.

Within minutes the train cars began moving back and forth, and rocking from side to side. We had entered the mountains of West Virginia. With the cars swaying from side to side on the uneven track, it was impossible to fall asleep in the small quarters. My mind drifted to thinking about home, my family and friends. Also, I tried to picture the young lady who occupied the sleeping berth across the way; I wonder if she was the young woman that got on the train in Charleston.

What seemed like only minutes of travel, the train had stopped again. I could hear the sound of footsteps outside the door of my berth. I rolled over and raised the blind slightly in the sleeping car and looked out the frost-covered window into bright morning sunlight.

I was not sure where the train had stopped, but I quickly glanced at my watch to discover it was 0730. To my surprise, I had fallen asleep for a couple of hours. I sat up, and while searching for my shaving-kit, swung my legs out from under the blanket and placed my feet onto the cold steel floor. The train started moving again as I stood up and walked naked to the small metal sinks.

Taking a towel from the rack, I wrapped it around my waist and opened the hot water faucet to find only a small stream of lukewarm water came forward. I splashed the water to my face and looked into the small, dirty mirror attached to the bulkhead above. A thin, sun-tanned face stared back at me. Picking up a razor, I scraped the soft stubble of a beard from my face and chin, leaving only a slight outline of a black mustache above my upper lip.

Within minutes I was ready to go to breakfast. Leaving the sleeping car, I walked forward passing through two, crowded passenger cars in route to the dining car. As I entered the dining car, I soon realized that there were people seated at all the tables.

This must be a popular time to have breakfast, I thought as I turned around to go back to where I remembered seeing an empty chair when I first entered the car. I excused myself as I stepped in front of one Porter pouring coffee, and then squeezed past a second one serving breakfast from a large, stainless steel tray.

"Are you having breakfast with us, Sir," asked the Porter.

"Yes, but it looks as if I'll have to come back a little later," I said glancing forward searching for a vacant seat.

"There is one just forward on your right, Sir. Unless of course the young lady is expecting someone to join her," the Porter stated as he pointed in the direction of the table.

As I approached the table, I said, "Excuse me, Miss, are you expecting someone to join you for breakfast?"

"No", she replied looking up from the menu. "Please have a seat; I really don't like dining alone anyway."

My God. It's her, the girl that got on the train last night in West Virginia, I said to myself as I pulled the chair back and sat down.

"Thanks. Thank you. It looks as if everyone is having breakfast at this hour," I uttered searching for words.
Remembering my first view of her boarding the train last night, she was even more

beautiful up close than I could have imagined. Her long, auburn hair gave off a ravishing halo in the early morning sunlight.

"Would you like to see the menu?" she asked directly. I could tell by the tone of voice that she was uncomfortable with my staring at her.

"Oh, I'm so sorry ... that was rude of me. Please accept my apology," I said, feeling quite embarrassed.

"Are you traveling on business"? she asked politely, trying to change the subject.

"No, I just joined the Navy and I am on my way to Boot Camp," I managed to utter.

"The Navy you say. I have a brother in the Navy. He is a pilot aboard an aircraft carrier, she said proudly as the Porter approached the table to take our orders.

"I'll have a small glass of orange juice, toast, and coffee with cream," she requested as she handed the menu to the waiter.

"And you, Sir. What will you have this morning?"

"Oh, I would like an order of scrambled eggs, coffee, two English muffins, and a glass of orange juice, please," I replied.

"Since we are having breakfast together, we should at least introduce ourselves, don't you think? My name is

Laura," she said while extending her hand across the small table.

"Yes, you are right. I am Lou, Louis Adams," I responded while offering my outstretched hand. As she extended her arm, I could not avoid catching a glimpse of her cleavage with her full, well-developed breasts, emerging from the bondage of a stretched, white bra partially exposed under a lovely, beige blouse that was trying to provide some coverage without the use of the top two buttons.

"And, how about you? Are you going to D.C. on business or for pleasure?" I asked, as I quickly glanced back to her face to avoid being caught again admiring her breasts.

"No, I work in Bethesda, Maryland, at the National Institutes of Health...the NIH, as it is called. I was just home attending my father's funeral. He died from complications following a heart-attack two weeks previous."

"Oh, I am sorry about your father," I replied, feeling a bit guilty for having mentally disrobed her minutes earlier.

"Thank you," she said. "He also had some pulmonary problems that were related to his earlier work in the coal mines. He chain-smoked cigarettes, like they were going out of style. Maybe two-and-half packs a day. Do you smoke?" She inquired.

"No, I don't smoke cigarettes. I did at one time, but I quit," I answered. "Well, that's good. I am afraid people do not really appreciate the long-term health problem related to smoking. Oh, I am sorry, I don't mean to lecture you about smoking. Let us enjoy our breakfast, shall we? Bon Appetite," she said with a smile.

"Right," I replied, as I raised my small glass of orange juice as if to offer a toast.

It was obvious to me by now that she not only was a beautiful woman, but one with style and grace. She was, without a doubt, a person with proper training and education. Certainly, she was a person who was "out of my class"

"A penny for your thoughts," she said, trying to renew the conversation.

"I was just wondering what kind of work you do at NIH. It was NIH, Right?"

"Yes, I am a clinical psychologist. I do clinical research in the Institute of Mental Health at NIH. It involves studies with small children who are referred to the Institute. And we do drug trials...to see what drugs are beneficial."

"That's very interesting. Then you are a doctor?"

"Yes, but I am not a physician; I have a PhD degree in psychology and I am in-charge of a clinical section where we do a lot of the studies. You will have to come and visit us sometime, when you are in Washington," she continued.

"Yeah, that would be very nice," I acknowledged. But, really, when would I have the opportunity to go and visit a doctor I had just happened to meet on a train. The chances were not that good for me to get away even if I wanted to see her sometime after my arrival at Bainbridge.

Maybe I could get a pass from training and go down to DC and see her? That was what I would really like to do. But, wait a minute, this can't be real. She was just being nice. She would probably never even remember my name if I did call her, let alone agreeing to go out together. This is just one of those chance meetings of a beautiful woman on a train that I had read about in Readers Digest, or was it the Saturday Evening Post?

"Is something wrong? You haven't taken a bite of your food and you have allowed it to get cold? Here, let me call the Porter and I will ask if he will warm it up for you. Especially the scrambled eggs," she said, while reaching across the table and gently touching my hand.

"No! No, that's all right. I guess I am not very hungry," I replied, before taking a small bite from an English muffin and a sip of cold coffee.

"Would you like a refill on your coffee," I asked, realizing that she had almost finished her breakfast, while I had been starring out the window and deep in a state of mental gymnastics regarding our possible future encounters.

"Yes, thank you. That would be great," she answered, as I turned around to look for the Porter.

As the Porter refilled our coffee cups, I again found myself admiring her lovely face. Finally, I gathered enough courage to make a comment. "I hope you will not be offended, but I think you have beautiful eyes and a lovely smile."

"Thank you; I am not offended at all. Thank you again for having breakfast with me. Please allow me this treat by paying for your breakfast," she said as she opened her purse and placed a twenty-dollar bill on the table.

"Oh, no, I can't allow you to buy my meal. I have a voucher for meals from the Navy for use during travel," I quickly replied.

"That's all right. You can buy dinner one evening when you come to Washington," she said as she took a business card from her purse and wrote on the back of it.

"This is my home phone number I am writing here, and you also have my office number and address on the front of the card. Please, give me a call when you have an opportunity to visit, and I'll show you around town."

She handed me the card, gracefully excused herself, and we both stood. As she smiled and turned to leave, I noticed that she was wearing a matching dark-blue skirt that was tailored short to be in style, but it was drawn tightly around her buttocks to be sufficiently revealing of her beautiful figure without being offensive.

Dumbfounded, I stood for a moment reading the card: "Laura Blackmon" [f], Clinical Psychologist." Could this just be a nice person returning to work in Washington, and it was only fate that had allowed us to meet? On the other hand, was it pure adolescent fantasy or was this the real thing? Like one of the characters in the many chapters from Uncle Barney's repertoire of awesome and wild stories he had told us about during his experiences while serving overseas in the U.S. Army during World War II? A chance meeting of boy meets girl in an exotic setting followed by a torrid love affair?

"Redheads are beautiful like other women only more so," I remembered Uncle Barney saying several years earlier. At that time, I was not sure of the meaning of those words. It had to be correct if Uncle Barney had said it. After all, he certainly knew about women in France, Italy, Spain, and even North Africa [11]. To hear him tell it, he and his Army buddies had made love to all the girls, and still had time to win the "Big One."

The journey from civilian to sailor began at the "Main Gate" leading onto the U.S. Navy's Recruit Training Center in Bainbridge, Maryland. Two-weeks after I passed through this Gate, brother Bert dropped out of High School and followed me into the Navy. He wasn't going to allow me to "have all the fun."

The six-week boot camp training went pretty well for both of us, even though we were separated and assigned to

a different Company on the same Base.
After the long hours standing cloth-line
and fire-watches in the middle of the night,
I can say that I learned to sleep standing
up, and I was not the only one. Also, my
Company was the only one marching back-
and-forth across the "Grinder" on
Thanksgiving Day in 1953.

I want to say that every morning in
boot camp, after PT and breakfast, we had
a formation and rifle inspection in front of
the flag pole before morning colors. To this
day, one of my favorite memories of the
Navy was standing there for morning
colors. I still remember the bugle call note
for note, and I loved watching my fellow
Sailors hoist the flag to the sound of
morning colors.

Recently, my grandsons have asked:

What is the toughest part of Boot
Camp? And, what is the purpose of Boot
Camp?

(f) I did see Laura again in 1987 while I was working
at the U. of Cincinnati. She was a member of a NIH
Site Visit Team that visited the University during a
grant review process.

******

CHAPTER 15

Hospital Corps School

After graduation from Boot Camp, Bert and I received Orders to different classes in Hospital Corps School at Bainbridge, Maryland. The curriculum included: Anatomy and Physiology; Biochemistry; Pharmacology and Toxicology; Preventive Medicine; Bacteriology; Chemical and Biological Warfare Agents; First Aid, Minor Surgery, and Emergency Procedures.

At the time, these were subjects that I felt would certainly offer me some academic challenge; but, after completing the course work that knowledge provided me an opportunity to discover that I wanted a career working in the biological sciences. Certainly, these early, basic studies would help prepare me for college after the Navy.

My first duty assignment as a Hospital Corpsman was "Night-Duty" in the Delivery Room in the Naval Hospital at Bainbridge. This night-duty crew was always busy, because it seemed that most of the mothers-to-be went into labor and had their babies at late night or in the early morning hours. Nevertheless, this was still a good duty assignment for Corpsmen because the young, good-looking Navy Nurses also had duty in the Delivery Room and in the Nursery.

When no one was in labor, it was a period of time that was usually spent cleaning surgical instruments, scrubbing down a room, or autoclaving new surgical packs. This was also a time when the work environment was less formal and it permitted more casual conversations among the Corpsmen and the Nurses. Moreover, it was always more difficult to maintain any semblance of formality when you were walking around, bending over, and working in close proximity to each other while wearing only your underwear and a scrub-suit.

This informal atmosphere was accepted and practiced by most of the staff in the Delivery Room, particularly by a Lieutenant Junior Grade (LT (jg)) Jane Parsons. Jane and I worked well together as a team and were competent. Occasionally we would find ourselves in the Central Supply Room, in the Prep-Room, having to go to the pharmacy or being scheduled to go to midnight-chow at the same time.

It was also during these particular times she teased me about my hairy-chest, or talk about how nice it would be to be stationed on the West Coast near the beach so we could take long walks after midnight, or a time that she could go swimming in a new two-piece bathing suit. She would use any occasion to again remind me that I had an open invitation to come over to her apartment to hear her Frank Sinatra record collection.

I dismissed these conversations initially as being friendly work-place chitchat. Nonetheless, one night while everything was relatively quiet with only one mother-to-be in early labor, the two of us strolled onto the back veranda of the Delivery Room. This was usually where one would go to "catch some fresh air," or where the smokers would go to have a cigarette. It was also not uncommon to just slip-away to this secluded area to catch a momentary view of the moon. This was where I first realized that our relationship had changed.

"I have a question I have been waiting to ask you all evening, but we have not had a real opportunity to talk," she began, as she walked over and stood very close to me.

"Oh, yeah," I replied innocently.

"Come on, now. Don't act so naive. Why have you been avoiding me lately?" She inquired, as she put her arms around my waist and pressed her firm, warm body against me. I could also see the outline of her beautiful face in the moonlight, as the smell of her perfume reminded me of fresh, spring flowers, and the sight of her slightly parted lips made her irresistible.

"What do you mean? I have not been avoiding you," I questioned, while taking hold of her arms and gently, but deliberately, pushing her away.

"We can't be doing this Jane. After all, have you forgotten that I am engaged to be married! I've told you about my girlfriend, and everything. What if we get caught doing this while we are on Duty! We'll both get a Captain's Mast; especially with me an enlisted man and you being an officer," I followed.

"I am not worried about getting caught. I just want you to know that I care about you," she continued, as she came close to me again with her head tilted upward.

Now, I could see tears flowing down across her pretty face. Without any regard for tomorrow, I pulled her tightly into my arms and began kissing her inviting lips. The pleasure of her warm embrace was more than I could have dreamed it to be.

Moments later, taking the back of my hand, I pushed her blonde hair aside, and gently wiped away the remaining tears from her face. Suddenly, the lights came on inside the Delivery Room nearby. We both jumped back and stood quietly in the shadows. Inside the prep-room we could see another nurse searching for something in a drawer of one of the stainless-steel cabinets.

Seconds later, she retrieved an instrument from the drawer, turned out the lights, and quickly retreated to the next room. We were relieved that we were not caught in our moment of indiscretion, and we just stood motionless, holding hands for a moment.

"Boy, that was close. We were almost caught!"

"I am sorry," she replied apologetically. "We just have to be more careful, that's all."

"Be more careful," I thought. What an enigma? I could now envision myself trying to explain why I was "Making-out" with one of the nurse officers while on Duty.

"No, we have to cool-it. This is not something we should be doing anyway," I said, trying to restrain my passion for her.

"We will see," she whispered, as we both retreated back into one of unused Delivery Rooms nearby.

The remainder of the early morning hours passed quickly with numerous exchanges of fleeting smiles between us. Officially, dating or any sign of overt intimacy between Corpsmen and Navy nurses was forcefully and enthusiastically discouraged by the "top brass" and senior Nursing Staff. However, it was common knowledge that two of our nurse friends had married Corpsmen during the first year I worked there. One nurse still worked in Labor and Delivery and the other one was on pregnancy leave from the Nursery.

Invariably, when the Chief of Nursing got word of one of "her nurses" dating a Corpsman, both of them soon received "Orders" to different duty stations several hundred miles apart. After all, the proud and unblemished U.S. Navy could not allow its Nurse Officers to fraternize with mere "Enlisted Corpsmen."

All the Navy Nurses below the rank of LCdr. were constantly reminded by the Top Brass that "Familiarity Breeds Contempt."

After, being removed from Night-Duty in the Delivery Room, I was mysteriously and abruptly transferred to Ward #801 in the same hospital at Bainbridge. One may say I got the royal shaft!

Neither of us ever received a clue as to who had surreptitiously contacted the Chief Nurse and who in turn had felt it was their duty and responsibility to separate the two of us. Jane stayed on "Night-Duty" and I drove her to work from her apartment in Havre de Grace, Maryland. in her car, each evening, which was about 10 miles from the base. Our relationship had become more significant for the both of us and we very much enjoyed being together.

On an occasional weekend, we visited the historical sites in the small towns nearby in eastern Maryland, and during one weekend we even traveled to Springfield, Massachusetts, to meet her parents.

Ward #801 was a "dirty surgery" ward that housed male patients who had gastrointestinal or G.I. problems. G.I. was a term that included surgery on patients with problems that extended from the stomach to the rectum... ulcers, pineal cyst, rectal bleeding, etc. Patients were admitted there post-operatively; however, the ward complement also included several older sailors who had developed ulcers following an extended period of alcohol consumption.

As for Jane, she unexpectedly received Orders to the Naval Hospital in

Portsmouth, Virginia. about two months after my assignment to Ward 801. She became very upset after learning of her pending transfer and even begged me to consider requesting a transfer to Portsmouth so we could be together.

One morning after she had worked all night and we were having breakfast together in the hospital cafeteria, she again inquired if I had gone to the Personnel Office and requested a transfer. After telling her I had not found the time off from my ward duties during the day to submit the request, she became very emotional and resorted to tears and accused me of not caring enough about her or our relationship to follow-up on such important issues. I also made the mistake of saying jokingly that she would be able to wear her two-piece bathing suit at nearby Virginia Beach even if I didn't get a transfer.

She immediately left the table in tears and said she was very tired, and that she was going to her apartment to get some rest and sleep. Stunned by her display of emotions, I took a couple sips of coffee and make my way to Ward 801. Later, at about 1000 during the morning, I received a phone call requesting that I report to the Chaplain's Office.

As I left the ward and walked down the long corridors leading to the Chaplain's Office, thoughts about a possible accident or sickness involving my parents or my brothers and sisters back home raced through my mind because that's why one gets a call from the hospital Chaplain. Something bad and unexpected had happened. Upon my arrival, I was met by the Chaplain, the Chief Nurse, and one of Jane's nurse friends, Lt. Jo Morgan.

The Chaplain began with a statement of fact regarding some bad news of a Navy Nurse involved in a train accident earlier that morning. "I regret to announce that the accident involved a nurse, a Ms. Parsons, and I understand she was a friend of yours, Lou," he continued.

"Yes; is she alright?" I inquired as the Chaplain took me by the arm and guided me to a chair nearby.

"No, I am sorry to report that her car was struck by a train while she was attempting to cross the railroad tracks near her apartment in Havre de Grace and she was killed instantly," he continued.

"No, it can't be," I uttered while trying to hold back my tears.

"I am so sorry, Lou," both nurses said as they tried to console me.

After the Memorial Services for Jane in the Base Chapel, her body was moved back to Springfield for burial. Because of the circumstances preceding her accident and death, I became very bitter with the Navy, the Chief Nurse, and myself. I was too young and immature to understand and appreciate our relationship and what it had meant to Jane. Admittedly, I did feel, for the first time in my life, a sense of deep affection for her.

While trying to make sense of my loss, I was reminded of a few words from a poem I had read earlier:

"Some people come into our lives and quickly go; some stay awhile and leave footprints on our hearts ... and we are never, ever the same.

*****

CHAPTER 16

Duty at Norfolk

After Jane's death, Bert and I requested transfers to the Naval Air Station (NAS) in Norfolk, Virginia. While waiting for our request to go through the chain of command, I went home on leave and got married to Betty in Richmond, Indiana. Even though I never admitted it to anyone, I was on the rebound and emotionally trying to recover from my personal loss.

After our arrival at NAS in Norfolk, I was assigned to work in Aviation Medicine, and Bert was assigned duty in the pharmacy and eventually to one of the wards.

The male Corpsmen's barracks was located over the Ambulance Garage and within walking distance of the hospital. The living quarters consisted of a large open room filled with metal bunk-beds. There were two candy vending machines, a well-stocked refrigerator, and two large card tables near the entrance to the room. There was a poker game or blackjack game in progress most nights.

There was no place for privacy and modesty within a men's barracks during the 1950's. Open showers were common and large enough to accommodate a crew of 35 men. Homosexuality was not tolerated and the "Don't Ask Don't Tell" policy came much later in the 20th Century.

Late one hot summer's night, laughter and girlish giggles coming from the bathroom or "Head" awakened me. I got out of my bunk to investigate. To my astonishment, I discovered that brother Bert and one of his buddies, along with two beautiful, nude females were taking showers together.

Half asleep, I proceeded to relieve myself in front of the urinal; then, I was casually invited to join in on the clean fun by one of the young ladies. I declined, and as I turned to leave, I saw two blue uniforms with small airline stewardess wings pinned to their lapels, and women's underwear that had been hastily draped across one of the chairs and on the floor outside the shower area. Apparently, the girls were part of a layover crew who had a few drinks, and they just needed a place to freshen-up a bit before their return flight home later in the day.

In addition to our regular duty assignments, periodically Corpsmen would catch a month of Night Duty. I was assigned to the ER and Bert was in the X-ray Department. During the day, instead of sleeping we would jump into my 1955, Black and White, Crown Victory Ford and head for Virginia Beach to build "Sand Castles" with the young college girls who were there on vacation. This made for a couple of tired and frequently sunburned individuals on Night Duty.

Life in the Navy for the Adams' Brothers was not always one of fun and games, however.

The hospital at the NAS in Norfolk consisted of four wards for inpatient care, but it had a large outpatient population who visited the various clinics from time to time. Patients who required elective surgery, or extended care were sent to the U.S. Naval Hospital in Portsmouth, Virginia. However, both male and female military patients, as well as dependents were seen in the Emergency Room 24-hours a day. It was here that Bert and I received a lot of experience suturing wound/lacerations during the evenings.

The Aviation Medicine section, where I worked during the day, was responsible for determining whether the airmen were physically and mentally fit for their aviation duties. This also included conducting studies of the effects of flying on the physical, mental, and emotional well-being of pilots during and after flight. The Flight Surgeon at the time was Dr. Roger Fowler.

Most of the work for me consisted of conducting annual physical examinations of the pilots and crew members. I was responsible for doing the preliminary examination, which included special eye and blood pressure exams and lab studies. Dr. Fowler did the physical examination and he sighed-off on the medical forms.

During the first six-months working in Aviation Medicine, was an especially busy period. This was shortly after Congress had approved the promotion of all the pilots who were former enlisted men and who had received temporary reserve appointment to officer rank (USNR) during the Korean War. After the War ended, they were reduced back to their enlisted rate of either First Class Petty Officer or to Chief Petty Officer [24]. History has shown, these were some of the Navy's best aviators [24,25].

Most were Test Pilots who had logged thousands of hours of flying, and many hours of combat time over Korea. They had the best flying skills, but they lacked one small item or "chit" in their Navy personnel records - a College Degree. Finally, Congress had acted on President Truman's recommendation and they were now to receive a permanent rank of either LT (jg) or LT. in the regular United States Navy.

I could identify with these men, because there were many occasions when I was made aware of my limitations without a college degree, even in the Navy! That was why I was taking evening college courses at William and Mary at night. I had often marveled at the fact the Navy had given a commission to several of my Navy Nurse friends after only three years of formal training.

Regardless, this was a great day for the pilots! I could tell during their physical examinations for promotion that this was a "Happy Group of Pilots." These men were finally going to receive the well-earned recognition and compensation for their past and current efforts in Service to their country.

It was also during these occasions that I would make arrangements with the various pilots to "hitch a ride" in the planes. The arrangements were usually made with the pilots in the "Overhaul and Repair section (O&R)", because they were the "Test Pilots" who had to "check-out" the planes after repair, and before they could be sent back to the squadrons for regular use on the flight line. They were usually former enlisted guys, with whom I had established a good "esprit de corps."

Whenever a plane was available for a "check-ride," the test pilots would try to schedule the flight during the noon-hour so I could go on the flight with them without taking time off from work. These little sorties became rather frequent and they were called "Nooners." During one such "Nooner" I had "hitched a ride" in an old, open-cockpit N3N, with former Chief Logan Bannon.

We were out flying south over Virginia Beach at about 4000 feet when Bannon turned the controls over to me. The old plane was moving along about 85 knots when suddenly, without warning, the engine started to "sputter" and "miss" like it was not getting fuel. Then, the windshield became covered with oil and smoke filled the cockpit.

"Well, nothing to worry about. We just lost an oil line! Here, I'll take her back in to the field," Bannon said as he took the stick and made a slow turn westward and back toward the field.

"Norfolk tower this Navy 168 Tango ... we are about 4000 feet and east of the field ... and we seem to have lost an engine and we're headed home. Request a straight-in approach on One-Zero," Bannon radioed without showing any sign of concern for what to me was rapidly becoming an emergency!

"Navy 168 Tango -- understand you have lost your engine. Are you declaring an emergency," the tower requested?

"No emergency here. Would like a straight-in - since I had to shut her down because of smoke in the cockpit," Bannon replied.

"168 Tango, you are cleared to land.'

As we made our "dead-stick" approach to the landing, on the ground I could see the fire trucks and the ambulance racing along the runway towards our plane as we touched down and rolled to a stop.

When we climbed out of the plane, Bannon turned to me and asked; "Are you alright, Doc"?

"Yes, I am okay. That was a good landing, Chief," I said.

"They are all good landings - as long as you can walk away from them, Son."

The fire truck routinely sprayed foam over the fuselage of the plane as a fire precaution, and this little incident of a "dead stick" landing did not discourage me from climbing back into another aircraft later in the week.

On any given night, Corpsmen were also scheduled on "Crash Crew Duty" which consisted of manning the Crash Ambulance in the event of an aircraft accident. For seaplane operation, an additional two Corpsmen were required to go out in the "Duty Boat" with the aviation crew to mark the sea-lane with buoy lights for seaplane takeoff and landings at night.

VP-56 was the Squadron of Martin P5M-1 Mariner amphibian aircraft based at NAS Norfolk at that time in the 1950's, and they were always flying at night. Most of the P5M-1s at Norfolk were used for Anti-Submarine Warfare (ASW) patrol off the East Coast and transporting supplies. Sometimes the planes flew a "milk run" to Bermuda. This was a way to stock the Officer's Club with good and inexpensive booze.

It was on one such occasion when Bert and I had made plans to hitch a ride on the "milk run" to Bermuda on the P5M-1 for a few days. However, on the Good Friday night before Easter, we were scheduled to leave, Bert was unable to secure someone to take his weekend ward duty. This being the case, I decided not to go on the flight either, but instead I relieved a friend from the "Boat Duty".

The "Boat Duty" required the crew to be in the sea-lanes by 2000 hours for a scheduled plane departure at 2200 hours. The purpose for the boat crew being out on the water early was to "sweep" the sea-lanes of floating rubbish and debris, as well as to ensure that the taxi and takeoff marker lights attached to the floating buoys were functioning correctly.

The task of clearing the sea-lane was uneventful, and about 2130 hours the P5M-1 left the dock and it was observed by the boat crew making its way north along the lighted water taxiway. At the end of the water taxiway, the pilots went through their preflight checklist; and, they were overheard by members of boat crew when one of the pilots radioed the tower to acknowledge they were ready for takeoff.

Clearance for takeoff was given, and at that point the pilot should have turned the aircraft to 90 degrees heading to start the takeoff run in an easterly direction that would have taken the plane out toward the Atlantic Ocean. Instead, the plane began the takeoff run at a heading of 180 degrees back down the water taxiway.

Since the "boat crew" did not have two-way communications with the pilots or the tower, we were left out of the communications loop and could not warn the pilots of their mistake. Moreover, due to the location of the tower on the field the air controllers did not have clear line of sight of the aircraft and they were unaware of the misdirection attempt at takeoff. Within minutes, the plane failed to gain sufficient altitude and crashed into the seawall.

Because the nose of the plane did manage to clear the seawall, the pilot and co-pilot were uninjured, but four of the eleven others aboard the plane were killed. Had it not been for the fact that Bert was unable to get someone to take his Duty; we would have "bought the farm!"

(See Addendum B below for an additional account of the accident).

*****

CHAPTER 17

Brothers Serve Together

The U.S.S. *Tarawa,* **Figure #3***,* was commissioned on 8 December 1945, three months after the surrender of Japan. It was named for the bloody Pacific amphibious assault against the Japanese defenders of an atoll named Tarawa in the Gilbert Islands during World War II.

It was in March of 1954 when brother Ed reported aboard the *U.S.S. Tarawa* at Naples, Italy. He had just completed Boot Camp and this was his first duty assignment. On board, the Tarawa got underway on a 74,260-mile around the world tour.

Now, there were three Adams' brothers in the U.S. Navy. Bert and I were at the Naval Air Station in Norfolk, Virginia, and we were ready for Sea Duty. With brother Ed at sea, we requested Orders to be with him aboard the *U.S.S. Tarawa.* If our requests were approved, the three of us would be stationed together.

Initially we were told that our request would be denied. The Navy was hesitant to assign more than two brothers aboard the same ship. The rationale for such a restriction was because of the loss of the five Sullivan brothers who were aboard the cruiser *U.S.S. Juneau (CL-52)* when it was sunk off Guadalcanal on 13 November 1942 during WW II [26]. The loss of those brothers has been called one of the greatest tragedies to any one family in U.S. wartime history.

The legacy of the Sullivan brothers was one of the oft-told stories of World War II, and subsequently a Hollywood movie entitled "The Fighting Sullivan's." The brothers, whose motto was "We Stick Together," stipulated as a condition of their enlistment that they be permitted to serve on the same ship. Even then, the brothers enjoyed a certain celebrity status for being the only five members of a family serving on one vessel.

Our motto was "We Serve Together!" Our reason for serving together was not one of seeking notoriety. It was to be our privilege and honor to serve our country; and, why not together? Approval finally came after the exchange of several official letters between the Bureau of Naval Personnel, the Captain of the *U.S.S. Tarawa*, and ultimately, a letter of approval from our parents. Our service together represented the first time three or more brothers from Ross County were in the military at the same time since the seven Purdrum brothers who served in the Civil War.

Bert and I reported aboard the *U.S.S. Tarawa* in September 1956 at Quonset Point, Rhode Island. I was overwhelmed by the size of the ship when I walked up the gangplank that day. I later learned it was almost three football fields in length and was capable of a speed of 33-knots under full-load displacement.

Ships' Company included 2,500 Enlisted Men and 240 Officers, who consumed 8,250 meals, 750 loaves of bread, 250 pounds of butter, 200 gallons of milk, and 550 pounds of coffee per day. The Ship had a library with more than 4,000 books, magazines and newspapers. I later learned it did more than 40, 000 pounds of laundry each week and it had a tailor shop, cobbler shop, and a print shop. Nightly movies were shown on the Hanger Deck along with Boxing matches. Other facilities included basketball courts, church services, lecture hall, and room for a parade ground.

Bert and I were both assigned to the Hospital or "H" Division, also known as Sickbay. "H" Division was an independently self-sustained and well-outfitted seagoing hospital; complete with Sick-Call and treatment rooms, aviation medicine physical examination room, laboratory, pharmacy, X-ray machine, and inpatient wards. Additionally, there were two complete operating rooms for any type of major surgery.

Our arrival brought the Medical Department to a full complement of 25 Hospital Corpsmen plus two Medical Officers. Captain Scanlan, (MC), a Flight Surgeon, was the senior Medical Officer, and Dr. Walter Deaton, LT. (MC) was second in command.

Over time I became competent in evaluating and screening patients for treatment; and, before long I was even permitted to do most of the suturing of wounds and lacerations that resulted from accidents aboard ship. These were duties only an intern, surgical resident or perhaps a well-trained physician assistant may be permitted to do in a civilian setting today.

Dr. Deaton and I worked together as a team and we frequently talked about what we were going to do when we got out of the Navy. Dr. Deaton had graduated from the University of North Carolina and planned to return home to complete a residency in Radiology. On several occasions, he had suggested that I should consider going to medical school after the service.

Bert routinely worked either in the 24-bed ward or in the pharmacy. The other Corpsmen were responsible for the Operating Room, Laboratory, X-ray, Flight-deck First-Aid Stations, General Quarters Battle Dressing Stations located throughout the ship, Administration Office, and the health records section.

In addition to sick-call and hospital care, the Corpsmen were responsible for the preventive medicine practices throughout the ship. Sanitation inspections of the "Mess-hall," and the "Berthing" areas, as well as, Biological, Radiological, Hazard Control surveys, and the teaching of First Aid classes that were routinely conducted by the Corpsmen. Specialized care was also provided in all aspects of Aviation Medicine. Chief Hospital Corpsman, Buffington, was the overall administrator.

Brother Ed was already working in "A" Division as an Engineer, when Bert and I reported aboard. Since Bert and I were working in Sickbay, Ed was assigned to be the responsible person for the maintenance and repair of the air conditioning units in Sickbay. **Figure #4** shows Bert giving Brother Ed a shot, while Brother Lou offers support.

At sea, the Flight Deck duty for the Corpsmen included "Standing Watch" during Flight Operations. In the event of an accident, the Corpsman would be the first medical person on the scene to render medical care.

The ship would leave Quonset Point and travel to various offshore stations and join other ships, including destroyers, supply vessels, and submarines. Once "On Station", the aircraft would be launched from the Flight Deck for "Carrier Qualifications" and simulated submarine "Hunt and Kill Missions."

Regardless of one's duties and responsibilities aboard this or any other aircraft carrier, we were all just support personnel and secondary to the real purpose of being---and that purpose was first and foremost the training of pilots!

During our tour of Duty on the *U.S.S. Tarawa*, we became world travelers; we traveled to the beautiful Caribbean on five different occasions. The Port of Call always included such exciting places as Port-au-Prince, Haiti; Kingston, Jamaica; and Gitmo Bay, Cuba.

During one trip to the Caribbean Sea, we assumed the Captain may have become lost because the ship anchored off St. Thomas and St. Croix in the Virgin Islands. This was "good liberty" because it was always exciting for the sailors to become "pseudo-tourists" and be allowed to enjoy the excellent bathing beaches, restaurants, hotels, and shops on these islands.

Ruins of castles and forts built by pirates during the 1700's were popular attractions. With the flurry of tourists on St. Thomas and St. Croix, the islands' spirit of relaxation appeared invincible. Additionally, a lonely sailor could frequently find a lovely lady and companionship among the many tourists staying at the hotels on those Islands.

During the long trips to sea, many of the Corpsmen played cards or worked on college correspondence courses during "off-duty hours" to help pass the time. Two evenings a week I ran the Ships' radio station (WTAR) as a disk jockey. I read the news and played records that were broadcast throughout the Ship and to our escort ships in the fleet over the Armed Forces Radio Network.

Another crusade on the *U.S.S. Tarawa* included "Joint Training Maneuvers" with the ships from the NATO countries in the North Atlantic Ocean in the late 1950s. In route, the Tarawa sailed through the Irish Sea to rendezvous with more than one hundred navy ships from many Allied Countries. In this main exercise, the Tarawa operated with the super-carriers *U.S.S. Forrestal* and *Saratoga*, as well as with the last of the great battleships, the *Wisconsin* and *Iowa*. This fleet operation represented the largest concentration of naval power since WW II.

Being at sea in the north Atlantic during bad weather in the winter months was not pleasant duty. Around-the-clock operations in inclement weather posed even greater demands on the skills of the flight deck crews and the pilots. Flight operations continued even during bad weather when the sea was always rough with 20-to 30-foot high waves that frequently cause the flight deck in the bow of the ship to go under water temporally. With the ship bobbing up and down like a cork, it became even more difficult and dangerous to recover aircraft returning from a sortie at night.

Bert had the duty on the Flight Deck on one such evening when several aircraft were being recovered for the purpose of "switching pilots." During such operations, the engines on the planes were not shut down and the propellers continued to rotate while the "old" crew disembarked, and the relief pilots climbed aboard the aircraft. The pilots were taught to move aft and away from the rotating props.

However, this was not the procedure attempted by one tired pilot who proceeded to try to walk forward between the rotating prop and the fuselage of the plane. Following that mistake, fragmented body parts, hair, pieces of flight-suit, and blood were distributed all over the flight deck, other aircraft, and several crew members. The only word from the "Air-Boss" was: "Get the flight deck cleared so he could recover aircraft."

The search of body parts and other fragments of human flesh was left to Bert and the other two Corpsmen who were called to duty on the flight deck. The Corpsmen collected the body parts, deposited them in a body-bag, and placed the bag inside a walk-in cold room below deck. Such responsible action was considered as part of their regular or routine duty.

It was during another trip to sea when the *Tarawa* was anchored out in the bay and travel ashore on Liberty and back to the ship was by a motor launch operated by a Coxwain and a Machinist Mate who ran the engine. On one return trip to the ship, a drunk sailor fell overboard. Brother Ed was on duty as the Machinist Mate. Without hesitation, he stopped the motor launch and dove into the water and pulled the sailor aboard... saving him from drowning.

This were the types of action taking place every day in the Navy to prevent accidents and serious injury to fellow shipmates. No heroics. Just performance of regular duties.

In the meantime, my marriage to Betty had unofficially ended while we were at sea. It was during this cruise that I received notice via mail that Betty had filed suit for divorce. Although not unexpected, the date for my response and appearance in court was fast approaching. Being at sea, the mail delivery to the ship via plane was infrequent and depended upon when and where we would reach the next port of call. After the ship docked in Plymouth, England, I called my friend and attorney Gerald E. Radcliffe in Chillicothe, Ohio requesting him to represent me in the uncontested divorce proceedings. In the final analysis, I had long subscribed to the old cliché that in marriage it was best to get it over early while you're young - just like chickenpox.

After the Ship's arrival, back in Quonset Point, we returned home for a visit with our family and friends. A 48-hour or 72-hour pass meant a quick return trip to Chillicothe, Ohio. This often-meant recruiting additional sailors as passengers to help defray travel expenses. All our travels from Norfolk, Quonset Point, or the Naval Shipyard in Boston to Chillicothe required trekking across some part of the Pennsylvania Turnpike.

Frequently heard from our fellow sailors as passengers was the constant grousing about the toll-booths, the construction crews who were ever present on the roadway, and the high price of hamburgers at the Howard Johnson restaurants in Valley Forge or at the Breezewood Exit. By any objective viewpoint, travel on the Turnpike was not one of pleasure, but it afforded an expeditious route home.

This turnpike was part of the massive highway construction in the 1950s during the Eisenhower Administration. For example, all states with enough gumption and sufficient pull in Washington, D.C.- began immediately building super-slabs. They all built fast-food restaurants that imitated the famous Turnpike's ham sandwiches, which could be either eaten, used for a new half-sole on worn combat boots, or for making a good head-gasket for your 1955 Chevy.

It was during one of these visits home that Ed wrecked my pride and joy- a black and white, 1955, Crown Victory Ford, following a night out on the town. Fortunately, he was not seriously injured, but the car was a total loss. I traded-in its remains for a white, 1956 Ford Convertible.

Within the next year, our time on Sea Duty was near an end, and we transferred off the *U.S.S. Tarawa*. Ed returned to civilian life, and within two weeks out of the Navy, he went to work at the Chillicothe Shoe Factory doing piece work on an assembly line making Red Cross shoes. Shortly thereafter, he was fortunate enough to be hired as a surveyor's apprentice doing major construction work at the Mead Corporation paper mill in Chillicothe.

While working at Mead he attended evening classes at Ohio University, married Marjory Brown from Frankfort, Ohio. They had two children, Kevin and Kimberley, and over the following years he continued to be promoted to several different divisions at Mead. His last assignment before retirement was Plant Manager of the Mead Forestry Division and Paper Storage Depot. Coincidently, this facility was one of the National Firework's bomb-making ordinance plants of 20-50 lb shells for use by the U.S. Navy during World War II. He retired from Mead in 1965 and lives on the Tecumseh High Plains Ranch and La Dolce Vita Vineyards near Chillicothe.

Bert and I re-enlisted in the Navy. While at home on leave and awaiting Duty Assignment Orders, I made a major mistake of using my shipping-over bonus monies plus the 1956 Ford as a trade-in on a 1957 Mercury convertible. Such immature action reflected my poor judgment and total lack of fiscal responsibility.

Bert was assigned to a Destroyer Tender, *USS Grand Canyon* (AD-28) out of Fall River, Massachusetts. This ship served as the Mother Ship to a squadron of six destroyers. Aboard were 16 Corpsmen and one physician. These medical personnel provided medical care to a crew of 2800 officers and enlisted men stationed aboard this ship; and provided medical services to those men aboard the destroyers

While on Liberty in Fall River, Bert met and began dating a young girl, Betty Lou Huffan. Two months later they were married in Warren, Rhode Island. Shortly thereafter, Bert was transferred to Shore Duty at the U.S. Naval Air Station at

Millington, Tennessee. Betty Lou was pregnant and remained in Rhode Island.

For Bert, the laid-back southern way of life in Tennessee was a welcomed change from the many years in the New England area. A few months later, William Bert Adams, Jr. was born on 1 August 1960. Unfortunately, soon thereafter, Bert's marriage ended leaving a long-standing void between father and son.

Within a few months after his divorce, Bert met a young WAVE, Joan A. Dore; and became smitten and a second marriage ensued. Duty in Memphis consisted primarily of Shore Patrol Duty which included 24-hours on and 24-hours off duty as the medical representative conducting blood alcohol tests, suturing wound lacerations and providing first aid to the wild, young sailors on Liberty. During his off-duty hours, Bert put his farm boy skills to work by acquiring a part-time job training horses at the local horse arena.

While training the horses, Bert ended up buying a big, fast, Paint gelding, named Sailor. They both did the cowboy-rodeo scene for a while (calf roping, barrel racing, etc.). Neither made the "big-time" and Bert kept his day job. He also kept Sailor, the horse.

During his stay in Memphis, a second child, Lavonne Kay, was born on 31 March 1962. Shore Duty ended with orders to advanced Independent Duty School at the US Naval Hospital in Portsmouth, Virginia. Bert, Joan, and baby Lavonne headed to Portsmouth via way of a short visit to Chillicothe, driving the old 1955 Mercury convertible, carrying a dog named Pepper, and towing a horse trailer hauling with Sailor inside.

In 1963, Bert completed Independent Duty School, a 14-month accelerated medical course that prepares Hospital Corpsmen to work independently from a doctor while deployed alone aboard a ship, with the Marines, or on a submarine. An Independent Duty Corpsman is responsible for the treatment of every medical condition imaginable—from arm fractures, appendicitis to heart attacks. So, when Bert was deployed aboard ship in future assignments, he had to make sure that the sailors were healthy, both physically and mentally, especially since many ships can be at sea for long periods at a time.

He gave immunizations, counseled the sailors, conducted health classes and maintained all medical records of all personnel on board. Diagnostic procedures, advanced first aid, basic life support, nursing procedures, minor surgery, basic clinical laboratory procedures, and other route and emergency health care were not beyond his scope of practice

After completing Independent Duty School, Bert was selected to attend Deep Sea Diving School at the Naval Gun Factory in Washington, D.C (NEC *8494)*.

While television and the movies seem to only focus on the sport of scuba diving, a very different kind of serious underwater operations by Navy hard-hat divers began early and has maintained a long and rich history of rescue and salvage activities. As long as there have been warships, navies have needed divers who could go underwater to make repairs, as well as salvage sunken or damaged ships.

After Diving School, Bert was transferred to the *USS Atakapa* (ATF-149), a fleet going ocean tug. The ship was named after the *Atakapa* native American Indian tribe found in Louisiana and Texas. Next, there was a need for a Corpsman with Hyperbaric Chamber expertise aboard the *USS Opportune* (ARS-41), a Rescue and Salvage ship out of Little Creek, VA. Service aboard the *USS Opportune* became his longest held duty station, lasting five plus years.

Travel included a World Cruise lasting 11 months. The duty included towing an HMS lifting vessel from Holy Loch, Scotland through the Mediterranean Sea, passing through the Suez Canal into the Red Sea, then onward to Vietnam, where he earned the Vietnam Service Medal. The cruise set two Navy records: the longest tow by another ship and second, the first submarine rescue and salvage ship to circumnavigate the globe.

In 1968, Bert received orders to the Naval Submarine Medical Research Laboratory in New London, Connecticut. Here his duties for the next two years included working as a diving instructor, medical researcher, and diving supervisor.

Following duty in New London, Bert was ordered aboard the *USS Skylark* (ASR-20), a submarine rescue vessel home based in New London. It was during this period of time Brother David reported aboard as a Seaman. As seen in **Figure #5**, Bert (l to r) extends a hand to his brother David in a jester of "Welcome Aboard" the *USS Skylark*. With David now in the U.S. Navy, this represented four of the six Adams 'Brothers' who had served their country in the U.S. Navy!

*****

CHAPTER 18

Duty at Bethesda & Camp Lejeune:

𝕴n 1957, I re-enlisted in the Navy for four additional years. As part of the agreement, the Navy assured me that I would receive orders to a facility where my interest in radio and TV broadcasting would be utilized. Earlier, while working as a deejay and reading the news aboard the USS *Tarawa,* I had acquired an interest in radio broad-casting as a possible career.

Upon my arrival in Bethesda, Maryland in early May, I was assigned to the new Medical Communications Division at the National Naval Medical Center (NNMC). At that date, the NNMC was a unique military medical complex. Larger than many nationally known corporations; the Center was, by size, among the ten largest medical facilities in the United States.

It was weeks later that I learned some of the history of the sprawling Medical campus. In 1938, Congress appropriated funds for the acquisition of some 400 acres of land for the construction of the NNMC. President Franklin D. Roosevelt chose the site on Wisconsin Avenue on 5 July 1938. At that time, the site was nothing more than a cabbage patch on a run-down farm.

President Roosevelt was particularly attracted to and interested in a small pond, fed by natural springs that was located on the farm. It was said that the pond reminded him of the biblical "Pool of Bethesda", which was a place of healing. The pond was later made into a small lake, and christened Lake Eleanor, in honor of Mrs. Roosevelt. In 1942, the NNMC consisted of a 1200 bed Naval Hospital, the Naval Medical School, the Naval Dental School, and a Naval Medical Research Institute.

I began on-the-job training behind a TV camera that broadcast on a Closed-Circuit Television System within the NNMC. It was not long until I realized that TV work was not the answer to my desire to work in medical science.

In June of 1957, I had an occasion to run into Cary Kirby at a *Senator's* baseball game. He was an old friend with whom I was stationed at the NAS in Norfolk, Virginia. Cary was an Instructor in the Laboratory Medicine Department at the Naval Medical School. After several beers at the Senator's Baseball Game in downtown Washington, we decided to have a few more drinks in one of the strip-bars on "N" Street before going home.

It was during our discussions when Cary suggested that if I was so disgusted with my TV work I should apply for Lab School. He assured me, that being on the faculty, he could "pull some strings" to get me into the next class.

Three days later, I received a phone call from Cary. He stated that he had arranged a meeting with Dr. William McFarland, the Director of Hematology Department at the School. The meeting went very well and three weeks later, I received orders to the next lab class. Classes began in September 1957. The old farm boy had been assigned to Laboratory and Blood Banking School at Bethesda, in Lab Class #29. Of interest, this was the same McFarland who first described the flagella, as a mode of motion of a lymphocyte *in-vivo*).

The didactic phase of laboratory school was a bit of a challenge at times, but I began to apply myself and my grades improved and I made a go of it. My personal life, on the other hand, deteriorated rapidly. I lived only to get drunk, chase women, and have fun with the guys. I even entertained the idea of dropping out of Lab School and requesting duty as a FMF Corpsman assigned with the Marines.

I felt I was the "Big Man on Campus" and I began to think I was too good for a future in a lab and just "rattling" test-tubes. Truth be known, I was being dishonest with myself and finding excuses to avoid facing reality.

I accepted a challenge offered by my buddies one Friday night at the Enlisted Men's Club. The dare was to remove the U.S. Flag from the flag pole in front of the Medical Center, and replace it with a pair of black panties collected from a Navy nurse friend.

At 0400, the lowering of the Ensign and the raising of the "Black Pendant" went off without a hitch. I further called a local radio station in Rockville, Maryland

and proudly announced that a strange and unique flag was flying over the Center. After the news crew arrived, photographs taken, the Officer of the Day (OD) awakened, wasn't long until I was ordered to report to the O.D.'s office.

Following denials from me and repeated threats of dismissal from school by the Administrative Officer, I later learned the panties were raffled off for charity by the Public Information Office on campus and, the whole affair quietly faded into obscurity.

The academic programs at Bethesda were heralded as some of the best in the nation, and the concentrated curriculum of laboratory training was said to be the equivalent to a 3-year college Medical Technology program. (I was later granted 12 hours of credit from this training program toward a degree in Biology by Ohio University).

The major reasons for the acclaimed reputation of the training program were due to two factors: 1). The student body consisted of well-trained Hospital Corpsmen who reported to class with an existing solid, basic medical background and most were seasoned personnel who had spent years working in hospitals, clinics, and some had battlefield experience from the Korean War; and, 2). The Instructors were top-notch professionals. The faculty included physicians, Allied Health Medical Service Corps Officers, (MSC), and outstanding senior enlisted personnel.

They all had strong academic credentials and most had clinical and research backgrounds. Each had published in peer review science journals, and many were considered leaders in their scientific fields. I didn't realize it at that time, but four of the teaching faculty members who taught classes during my tenure as a student, would have an even greatly influence on my life in later years. One of the notable persons was Chief Hospital Corpsman (HMC) Denner Kadel Lawless, Sr. After attending high school and college in Iowa, he enlisted in the U.S. Navy, where he spent 20 years of research in parasitology and tropical medicine, specializing in Malaria research. After retiring from 20 years in the Navy, he taught and furthered his research efforts over the next 10 years at the National Institutes of Health (NIH). Throughout his long scientific career, he was a prolific writer and published over 100 scientific papers in peer reviewed scientific journals [27-43]. **Figure #6**. D.K. Lawless and his wife Margaret in 1948.

He taught parasitology and he drilled the names of parasites into our brains by using respective pronunciation. To name a few, we learned the names of the Malaria parasites and their life cycle, nematodes, and other common parasitic in humans and animals.

During the didactic phase of studies, Chief Lawless would occasionally assemble the class in the early afternoon at the old "Country Store," a local watering hole located about four miles north of the campus on Rockville Pike. Here, we would take over the joint and hold class. He would stand in the middle of the room and have us call out the names and spelling of parasites. Although it may be a non-traditional setting by today's standards, the informal ambiance was acceptable and conducive to learning for this group of students.

Earlier in his naval career, Lawless had made many of his scientific discoveries while working with the U.S. Naval Preventive Medicine and Research Unit #3 (NAMRU-3) in Cairo, Egypt; and, those findings have subsequently contributed greatly to our understanding of how parasites affect human health. To his intellectual credit, he was also an amateur archeologist; and, his archeological findings were later donated to the University of Maryland.

Today, even after the "Arab Spring," NAMRU-3 remains a premier U.S. Navy research bio-safety level 3 enhanced (BSL-3E) laboratories with extensive human and animal viral diagnostic capacity located in the near east. It is one of the largest medical research laboratories in the North Africa-Middle East region and is also the regional influenza reference laboratory for the Eastern Mediterranean Regional Office (EMRO) of the World Health Organization (WHO) with close ties to the influenza laboratory at the U.S. Centers for Disease Control and Prevention (CDC).

The second enlisted man was HMC Joseph Baranski. Joe was a clinical bacteriologist who taught me clinical bacteriology at Bethesda. While later stationed at the U.S. Navy Preventive Medicine Unit No. 7, (PMU-7), in Naples, Italy, he provided medical services for the U. S. Sixth Fleet in the Mediterranean area. He and Commander Arthur King (MSC) were most helpful to me with conformational bacteriological assays of laboratory samples collected during an enteric diseases outbreak in Morocco [44]. He later retired from the faculty of the George Washington University School of Medicine as a Professor of Medical Microbiology.

Two other instructors whom I greatly admired were Drs. Arthur "Art" King and James J. Humes. Art King was a Medical Service Corps Officer (MSC) who also taught me microbiology. His easy going and mild mannered personality made learning clinical bacteriology a pleasure and his teaching skills formed an every-lasting atlas of diagnostic microbiology nomenclature in every student's mind. Art later, with Chief Baranski, provided scientific support to me in Morocco.

Dr. James J. Humes trained me in gross anatomy and autopsy procedures in the Pathology training phase of laboratory school, and I assisted with autopsies on many occasions. He, along with two other Pathologists, later attained immense unsolicited international fame by having the unfortunate task of performing the autopsy on President John F. Kennedy in November 1963 at the NNMC [45].

The Medical School offered other allied health training programs, including Physical Therapy (PT), Occupational Therapy (OT), Pharmacy School (Ph. S), and Chemistry School (CS) on campus. After classes, many of the students across campus participated in intramural sports. One such student who was in PT School was a young sailor by the name of Bill Cosby who played fast-pitch softball.

I was the starting pitcher on my Lab #29 team; and we had established a winning record that year... a winning record until we played Cosby's team. It was during that final innings that Bill knocked in the winning run. Yes, he was the same Bill Cosby who later became one of America's best-loved comic and media personalities.

It has been said repeatedly, even though you may not be aware of it at the time that many of your life-long friendships were established while serving in the military. At this point in my personal life, I had hit rock bottom! I had received a visit from the "Repo Man" for non-payment of the loan on the new Mercury, and I was in debt to several buddies from poker games and losses from bets made in football pools.

In retrospect, I needed a "swift kick" in the butt, to grow up, and to get my head on straight! If someone had suggested this at that time such advice would have been met with resistance, disdain and contempt. Nonetheless, thanks to a father-to-son-talk with Chief Lawless, who saw some promise of success, I remained in school and my grades gradually improved. Before graduation, I took the civilian examination and became a registered Medical Technologist.

Then, one morning at breakfast I had an occasion to see a new, young lady in the cafeteria. She caught my eye as well as that of several of my buddies who were seated several tables away. After several remarks among us about her refreshing beauty, I made a bold statement that surprised even my buddies: "That young lady doesn't know it yet, but I'm going to marry her."

This comment prompted some laughter and giggles from my buddies who were ready to dismiss any such serious remarks coming from their old rogue friend and classmate as pure balderdash.

Later during the day, I placed a phone call to Ms. Dora Honen, another one of my friends in the WAVE Barracks, inquiring as to the name of the new arrival at the Medical Center. Dora refused to tell me her name and stated that: "I should stay away from her because she was too young, naive and innocent for me to morally corrupt!"

She was later introduced to me as Shirley Patricia Cannon or "Pat" one evening during a double date at the Hot Shopps in Bethesda. Little direct conversation transpired between the two of us that evening. However, I now had a name to go with the face of a young lady whom I had discovered to be more attractive than she had first appeared from a distance that morning in the cafeteria.

Over the next week, I mustered enough courage to call Ms. Shirley Patricia Cannon for a date - she reluctantly accepted. Over a short period, the two of us became inseparable. For the first time, I had met someone that possessed class, exceptional beauty, elegance and intelligence. These attributes were foreign to the old rogue and farm boy from Ohio.

Shirley had joined the Navy following high school graduation from Anne Arundel High School near Fort Meade in Odenton, Maryland. Military service was a natural selection for her and she had professional aspirations of becoming a nurse; and, in fact had already been selected into Nurses' Training at Duke University in North Carolina under a special program sponsored by the Navy.

She was also an Army brat, who was born in Denver, Colorado, attended high school in Germany, and had earlier traveled throughout most of Europe. Her father, Walter, was a career soldier, her mother Lucile was a 1st Lieutenant in the Army Nurse Corps, her brother Ted was in the U.S. Air Force, and brother Philip, would later join the U.S. Army and become a veteran with service in Vietnam.

Early in our dating relationship, I was a guest in the Cannon household on many occasions. Both Shirley and her parents always made me feel welcome in their home. However, as time passed, I continued to struggle with the fact I felt intellectually inferior to Shirley, and I tried to retain her interest by being a braggart, and at times told outright falsehoods regarding my parents, my birthplace, and my social-economic status.

These adolescent shenanigans brought on due to a major inferiority complex proved to be unnecessary and very counter-productive in our relationship. Over time, these immature acts were injurious to our relationship and eroded her confidence and trust in me.

Albeit, I had still tried to portray myself while with my buddies as being detached and not serious in my relationship with Shirley; the truth was I had fallen in love with her. I had told my good friend Malcolm David Foster, a Lab School classmate, how I felt about her, but I had difficulty conveying or verbally expressing my feeling of love and affection to her directly.

This inability to express feelings was a trait I had long shielded since childhood. At no time in my youth did I observe any overt expression of affection between my mom and dad. This is not to say they didn't care deeply about each other, after all they had eight children!

My feeling of love for Shirley became obvious to my Mom during a visit at home with family during a brief Christmas vacation in 1958. I was at a total loss not being with her; so much so, I left my family in Ohio on Christmas Day to return to Maryland to be with her.

We were married in the Base Chapel at Fort Meade, Maryland on 28 June 1959, three days after my graduation from Lab School. Following graduation, I received orders to Fleet Marine Force (FMF) training (NEC 8404) in Camp Lejeune, North Carolina. The Navy came through again!

FMF training for Corpsmen was offered at Camp Johnson on Montfort Point, a satellite camp on Camp Lejeune. I received eight weeks of specialized training in advanced emergency medicine and the fundamentals of Marine Corps life, while emphasizing physical conditioning, small arms familiarity, and basic battlefield tactics. Although a Corpsman only carries his first-aid kit and a Colt 45 while on the battlefield, he is always responsible for the health of his fellow Marines. (See Addendum C).

The Base bordered the cities of Jacksonville and Wilmington, on Cape Fear River, and was the largest deep-water port in the state - and Wilmington was the birthplace of Whistler's mother. Other noteworthy persons from the Tar Heel State include Andy Griffith, Ava Gardner, and Dr. Walter Deaton, my former medical and military colleague from aboard the *U.S.S. Tarawa*.

After completing FMF School, I was transferred to the Naval Hospital at Camp Lejeune, North Carolina. By this time, Shirley was out of the Navy and we were assigned base housing at 3125 Bougainville Dr. in Tarawa Terrace, near Jacksonville. At work, I was in-charge of the Chemistry Section in the laboratory at the Naval Hospital.

My first boss and director of the laboratory was Dr. Frank G. Steen, LCDR, (MC), U.S.N. Dr. Steen graduated from McGill University in Montreal, Canada, joined the US Navy, and completed his medical pathology specialty training at Portsmouth, Virginia. Prior to going to medical school, he had served briefly as a Hospital Corpsman in the Canadian Navy.

As lab director, he was an excellent role model for the young Corpsmen under his command. Off duty, I frequently served as a crew member aboard his 16-foot sailboat. We entered several Rebel Class regattas and usually came in first or second during my tour of duty at Camp Lejeune.

Coincidently, several years later while I was with the Peace Corps, I learned Dr. Steen was promoted to Rear Admiral in the Medical Corps, and he was the director of all the schools at the NNMC in Bethesda, Maryland. He was most helpful to me by providing some continuing education materials for use by the Peace Corps Volunteers (PCVs) in Morocco [46].

William S. "Bill" Schrader, LCdr. (MC) USN, relieved Dr. Steen at Camp Lejeune. He was also my pathology instructor at Bethesda. Throughout our duty together he encouraged me to study for advancement, and to enroll in science related correspondence courses. He repeatedly encouraged me to apply for a commission in the Medical Service Corps

(MSC). He was also aware that I wanted to get out of the Navy after my next Sea Duty obligation and go to college. Both he and Dr. Steen saw some promise of a bright future within my reach providing I put forth the effort required.

Darrell was born on 3 Jan 1960 in the Naval Hospital where I worked. I can say without reservation that was one of the most rewarding and happiest days of my life. Every man longs for a son and I was blessed with my first son. Yet, being a father can be the most treacherous and challenging job a man can have. There are no guidelines to follow and no standards to go by and meet...trial and error are the rules of the road for new fatherhood. Risks are great and any immediate evidence of success is rare.

I admit now that I was frightened and inexperienced; and, I stumbled through early fatherhood until I gained my bearings and some responsibility as a man. Shirley was more mature and her maternal instincts kicked in quickly. She became a good mother to our newborn child. As for me, I was honored to have watched him grow, from an infant, toddler, little boy, teen, and now a man. He brought much needed focus into my life. He and I helped each other grow---he came to me at the most unsettling time in my life.

During his first two years of life, Shirley's father, Walter, made Darrell one of the most photographed children in existence. Being an amateur photographer, he enjoyed taking pictures of his new

166

grandson during our all too infrequent visits to Maryland. In early stages of a child's life, parents understand that their young children are like sponges and they soak up everything they experience and observe. This certainly was the case with Darrell.

Darrell later attended kindergarten with several young friends in a French school while we were in Rabat, Morocco. Upon our return, stateside, he completed elementary school, graduated high school from Walnut Hills, a college prep school, and entered the University of Cincinnati with an expressed ambition to make his "first million dollars prior to turning 30 years of age."

However, every father should remember that one day his son will follow his example instead of his advice. And, the road along life's highway frequently has many unexpected bumps and turns. Darrell got married, dropped out of college, and soon had a child of his own; our first granddaughter, Christina Marie.

On the 17 of May 1962, Dianne Caprice Adams was born in the same Naval Hospital as Darrell. She was a lovely, young lady with exceptional large, dark brown eyes. She weighed seven pounds and measured 22 inches in length. At 6-weeks of age she had completed her immunizations, including the smallpox vaccination in preparations for our trip overseas to Morocco. As I rocked her to sleep one night, I remember what my dad said: "A daughter may outgrow your lap but she'll never outgrow your heart." I also remember my mother repeating the old Irish sayings that went something like: "A son is a son till he takes him a wife, a daughter is a daughter all of her life."

Caprice survived our adventure in Morocco with the Navy and the Peace Corps [46], graduated high school in Cincinnati, and eventually graduated from the University of Cincinnati with a degree in Sociology. While a student there she met and married James A. Warren. They subsequently had four boys: Blake, Shane, Grant, and Kyle.

*****

CHAPTER 19

On the Road to Morocco

"Ahab the Arab" was a popular song during the summer in 1962; it was at the top on the "Hit Parade." There was a bit of irony associated with the song and a real coincidence that by the end of June, I had received orders to the Naval Air Station in Kenitra (Port Lyautey), Morocco; a faraway country that was still known and referred to by some as "French Morocco." To others however, when told of my new orders, they had mistaken Morocco with Monaco, and in turn requested that we were to be sure to say hello to Princess Grace and Prince Rainier for them.

Upon receipt of orders the Navy had provided us with some orientation reading materials about Morocco covering the geography, climate, the language, and some limited information about the government. However, a crowning moment for U.S. nuclear superiority came during what was later called the "Cuban Missile Crisis" of 1962 when Soviet Premier Nikita Khrushchev and President Kennedy had a bit of a disagreement and my transfer to Morocco was put on hold.

This was the closest the world had come to a nuclear war. The Soviets had installed nuclear missiles in Cuba, just 90 miles off the coast of the United States. Our military was placed on their highest state of readiness, and this included the Marines at Camp Lejeune. Soviet commanders in Cuba were authorized to use tactical nuclear weapons if invaded by the United States during the Bay of Pigs incident. The fate of millions hinged upon President Kennedy and Krushchev to reach a compromise. Fortunately, I did not receive orders to be reassigned with the Marines; however, I was told to "stand ready" as part of a possible invasion force to go to Cuba.

My original Orders were reissued and the Adams' family prepared for departure from the secure and shielded boundary of the United States for what was to become a unique journey into a region of the world that at first glance represented a mammoth step backwards in time. This was a journey to a country, where as travelers, we were without an effective sense of the diversity of the area. As for me, I lacked an understanding and appreciation of the cultural and historical background of the people

Nevertheless, Shirley and I spent time reviewing the pamphlets during our long flight overseas. The one thing that continued to race through my mind was the fact Morocco was described as a primary Arab country with a constitutional monarchy government and it was located at the northwestern corner of Africa. I could only vaguely recall from world history class that the structure of governments under a monarch was a hereditary arrangement whereby the king or queen had sovereign control over their people. (See Addendum D for history).

At the time, I learned these facts, the information appeared so dry, too remote, and far removed from the realm of any knowledge necessary for a farm-boy in Ohio. Little did I know back then while seated in a classroom, that one day the need for such information would be important and useful. Now, reading about Morocco, the information that impressed me most was the fact that although agriculture supported 70% of the population, but phosphate export accounted for 70% of the gross national product. My interest in agriculture was a direct reflection of my rural life on a farm and membership in Future Farmers of America (FFA).

Cities such as Casablanca, Marrakech and Tangier were only names that were occasionally mention in the news and more frequently in the movies. Only then, any lasting association with these cities was in the context of a movie setting such as "Casablanca," or as part of the story line in some book that was always filled with a tale of conspiracy and foreign intrigue. I was reminded of a book by Aleko Lilius entitled "Turbulent Tangier." It was filled with such amusing stories about the city when it was an international zone before Morocco got its independence in 1956 [46,47].

As with most Americans, Morocco was a distant, remote, and vague area of the world. And at best, Tangier was on the extreme northwest coast of Africa at the portals of the Mediterranean Sea where the long surges of the Atlantic rush through the narrow strait of Gibraltar.

To those, such as my Uncle Barney, who was with General Patton when they made their landings during "Operation Torch," [48-51] and passed through nearby Casablanca in route to the Allied invasion of Europe in WW II, Morocco was a hot, dry and dusty place, inhabited by men dressed in long robes and large turbans wrapped about their heads from material that appeared to be rolled, white bed sheets. To some, they were the dark-skin people who sat in fly-infested cafes on the outskirts of military bases drinking endless glasses of hot, sweet, mint tea, smoking pipes or self-rolled cigarettes filled with hashish, and uttering a bewildering language.

Still others who were more knowledgeable and may have served there in the Foreign Service since WW II or during The Cold War realized that Kenitra (formally Port Lyautey) had its own important history pertaining to the United States [52-54].

Caprice and Shirley were tired after the 18-hour flight from New Jersey to the Azores, then to Rota, Spain, and finally on to Morocco. Darrell, seemed to tolerate the long journey without difficulty. The plane arrived at the Naval Air Station in the middle of a hot, Sunday afternoon in June 1962.

When we stepped from the plane onto the tarmac, the heat from the sun would have been unbearable except for a slight, westerly breeze that came in from the nearby Atlantic Ocean. There were only a few people inside the terminal building, and the Coffee Shop was closed this Sunday afternoon. Most of the people present, except the Terminal Crew, were dressed in civilian clothing and they were there to welcome the new arrivals.

As we gathered at the baggage-counter, a voice came from the small crowd of greeters: "Are you folks the Adams family?" "Yes...yes, we are." I replied, extending my hand to one of the men who emerged from the small crowd. "My name is Kirkpatrick, and this is my wife Joan...and this is one of our daughters, Susan," he said, as we shook hands. "And this is Shirley, Darrell, and the baby is Caprice," I recited as we continued to exchange greetings. "How was your flight... a bit exhausting for the children, I guess?" he asked, as he placed his Sherlock Holmes- like pipe back into his mouth.

"Not too bad...a little long and rough on the baby," I explained. "Well, we are here to welcome you to Morocco, and we will also serve as your "Sponsor," he said as he picked up one of six pieces our luggage. "The job of a Sponsor is to get you settled-in, and to introduce you to some of the Moroccan customs you will face while you are living "Off-Base." As soon as the rest of your luggage arrives, we will take you to your hotel, and, tomorrow I will pick you up and take you to the Base," Kirkpatrick continued.

We proceeded to get into a small line to have our passports checked and stamped with the official seal of the Moroccan Immigration and Customs Services. "How long will it take before our car arrives from the States," I inquired. "Oh, it will take about six-weeks or more before you will get it; it depends on to where it was shipped to in Morocco...if it arrives in Casablanca, it may get here in six, but if you have to go to Tangier...it may take a little longer. It all depends on to where it comes in," he said with a smile. "Don't worry, we will provide you with any transportation you will need until your car arrives."

"What is your job, here on the Base?" I asked, as the car started the short journey to our hotel. "Oh, I am sorry, I am in-charge of the lab in the Base Hospital ...where you will be working. We will go right by there on our way," he replied as the car climbed the small hill leading to the main road that passed across the Air Station. Along both sides of the palm tree-lined street were large, two-story, white adobe-like buildings with flat roofs.

"Now, on your right, you can see the Base Chapel, the PX, and the Commissary. Across the street is, there ... the one with flagpole in front, is the Administration Building. And, on top of that little hill...on your right...is the Base Hospital. That's where you will be working during your tour of duty in Morocco," the Chief explained during our quick motor trip across the Base.

Within minutes, we were at the back-gate of the Base, which was manned by a U.S. Marine and a Moroccan Army sentry; both in Dress Uniform. "That is strange, you have guards on the gates in uniform. We were under the impression, because of the Cold War problems that our government was trying to downplay U.S. Military presence here? Isn't that why we are required to wear civilian clothing when we go off-base?" I inquired.

"Yes, that's true... it is really a Moroccan base, as far as anyone outside is supposed to know. We are in the process of turning it over to the Moroccan government and we are called "Advisors." As you will find out, there are many things that go on here that may seem a little strange," Kirkpatrick said, as we continued across barren land, passing a heavily-laden burro with two large burlap-like bags and a bearded man in strange-looking clothing astride his back.

"Oh, by the way, there are other U.S. Navy people stationed here at the two Communications Stations...one just outside of Kenitra in Sidi Yahia, which is a communication Receiving Station. This is where all radio traffic is received from Washington. That information is passed on or re-transmitted to all the U.S. ships in the Mediterranean Sea, NATO head-quarters and/or to our Embassies in Europe, via another Communications Station located in a small village called Bouknadel. Also, there are two U.S. Air Force Bases that are being phased out; one is at Sidi Slimane and the other one is Nouasseur," Kirkpatrick continued.

We entered the hotel through a small, iron-gate that allowed passage through a seven or eight-foot-high stone wall that surrounding a beautiful, well maintained courtyard. An iron balcony overlooked a small fountain in the center of a flower garden and a grove of orange trees. The hotel seemed out of place in Africa, because the architecture was typical of what one would find in the South of Spain, near Granada or Seville. It was then I remembered this was consistent with the fact the Ottoman Empire extended from Africa across Spain, Eastern Europe, and into USSR.

After checking in, the Kirkpatrick's helped carry our luggage to the two small rooms that were located on the second floor which were to be our living quarters for the next six momentous weeks. This stay included an introduction to the older European style public bathrooms, which were located down a long hallway and away from the main living area.

The hotel also contained some facilities and fixtures such as a Bidet (pronounced Bee-Day), a low bathroom plumbing fixture resembling a toilet commode but equipped with a spray or jet of water, used for washing the genital and anal areas. Such fixtures, I learned, were unique to European homes and hotels and not often seen in America.

It wasn't just the architecture and bathroom plumbing that appeared different, strange and out of place, it was the clothing, language, and the contrast in customs and culture as well. For a Westerner, it was like stepping "through the looking glass." To use the metaphorical expression, it was similar to the twilight zone, where nothing is quite what it seems, like being in a strange parallel world.

Looking through the Hotel's iron gate onto the street, we saw women and men passing by in their conventional dress called a "djellaba;" a long hooded garment made of wool or cotton with full sleeves. It had a hood that came to a point called a "qob" that was said to protect the wearer from the sun or in colder climate, like in the nearby Atlas Mountains. Here, the qob would keep in body heat and protect the face from falling snow.

However, in contrast to their parents, many of the children were wearing clothing very similar to that worn in the States. Also, unlike their mothers, most young Moroccan women were not wearing a veil, though they may wear a headscarf. We later learned that women also wear a Caftan or Kaftan, which is particularly decorated with embroidery and has openings for arms. They are usually worn on festive occasions such as at weddings, however. Men wore a red cap called a "Bernousse," that was more commonly referred to as a Fez by the Americans

Occasionally, we would see another heavily-laden donkey or burro with two large burlap bags and a bearded man wearing a djellaba and a strange-looking headscarf or turban astride his back. There was no bridle or rains to guide the animal, just the gentle respective tapping on the neck with a small stick was sufficient to get them both home for the evening.

While we were living in the Hotel, we got to know the Spanish proprietor and were introduced to his family. He had a young, teen-age daughter who made friends and played with Darrell in the courtyard during the day because the weather was nice. The temperature in Kenitra during the summer ranged from 76-84 degrees F. The exception being when the wind shifts to a flow from the Sahara Desert, then it can get extremely hot during what is called a "Sirocco." The coldest temperature was about 55 degrees F in January with a lot of rain, no snow.

Shirley boiled water to make Caprice's formula. We did not use the tap water and this was before the days of bottled drinking water. We were cautioned against getting it into our mouths when we bathed. She also soaked some of the locally purchased vegetables and fruit in a mixture of bleach and water before serving them. Fear of becoming ill from contaminated foodstuff was not only an individual issue for each new arrival, it became a greater public health problem as time went by. These were some of our new experiences with what has been coined "Culture Shock." An experience one may have when one moves to an environment which is drastically different from one's own.

During the first two days, I attended what was referred to as "Orientation Classes." I was instructed not to carry large sums of American money in my billfold or try to use our currency in any transactions off Base. And, we were told never carry more than $2 in any one place such as shoes, pockets, or pants cuffs. On the other hand, we were told we were also serving as unofficial "Good Will Ambassadors" and our interactions with the Moroccan people represented an opportunity for "Culture Exchange."

Chief Kirkpatrick came by each day and gave me a ride to the Base. He served as the Lab Director and he handled all the administrative details. He was also responsible for the small Blood Bank operation during the day. On-Call Duty in the lab was a 24-hour period, and this occurred every third night in rotation. Being the new man in the lab, I was assigned to the bacteriology section.

After about six-weeks in the hotel, we moved into a small white-washed, two-bedroom villa on Rue Homain el Fetwaki in Kenitra. There was no central heating. There was a fireplace in every room except the kitchen. The house and garden were enclosed by an eight-foot cement wall.

In addition to the "protective wall," I was convinced by an American friend living at Madeira Beach we should have a dog for additional security. So, I was talked into getting a large German Shephard that answered to the name of "Chris."

After a week or so of acclamation to the place, the dog would stay in the courtyard, but he would climb upon the edge of the wall and bark at the Moroccan passersby in the street. I did not think he was overaggressive, but one day he bit Darrell on his right cheek, leaving a one-inch scar on his face. Both Shirley and I became furious at the dog, so I took him to the Marines on Base for use as a Guard Dog.

Shopping for food was usually done at the Base Commissary, but occasionally Shirley would venture into one of the Souks (open marketplace) in the Medina (old part of town). There were no shopping malls or food stores like Kroger's or Sam's Clubs in Morocco at the time we were there. Each area in a souk specialized in a certain type of product, like clothing, jewelry, carpets, meats, and spices.

Moroccan cuisine includes dishes like couscous, tajine, pastille, and others. Spices such as cinnamon are used in cooking as well as sweets like Halva are very popular. Cuisines from neighboring countries also influence the country's culinary traditions. A Tajine pot is a conical shaped cooking container used to cook stews (lamb, chicken, pigeon, quail, fish or beef) braised under a low temperature.

Moroccan cuisine is rich with herbs and spices including: cinnamon, saffron, ginger, paprika, pepper, salt, cumin, chili powder, and turmeric. Other ingredients used in tajines may include preserved lemon, lemon juice, olives, olive oil, Argan oil, prunes, almond, fresh local vegetables, raisins, apricots, honey, dates, nuts, parsley, and garlic.

Dealing with language was frequently a problem. The official language was Moroccan Arabic, a dialect of Classical Arabic, however, French was also the recognized business language and Shirley held her own speaking French. Berber language was spoken by a large majority of native Moroccans. However, due to its proximity to the southern coast of Spain, many people in the northern regions of Morocco spoke Spanish, while English and German were often spoken in popular tourist destinations.

Our car arrived and we were slowing moving about the countryside-- a rare drive to Rabat to view the Capital City or a Sunday afternoon trek to Mehida Beach to play in the sand. We were getting out mingling with the people, discovering that Morocco was a "Country of many Contrasts."

Once we began interacting with the Moroccans, we discovered them to be very friendly. There were several unique customs that as Americans we did not appreciate. Among those were obligations for Muslims to pray five times a day - at dawn, noon, afternoon, sunset, and evening. The exact time was listed in the local newspaper each day. Friday was the Muslim holy day. Everything was closed. Many companies also closed on Thursday, making the weekend Thursday and Friday.

During the holy month of Ramadan, all Muslims must fast from dawn to dusk and are only permitted to work six hours per day. This, we learned from our Fatima and Gardener who worked two-days a week at our villa. Fasting included no eating, drinking, cigarette smoking, or gum chewing. Expatriates were not required to fast; however, they were requested not eat, drink, smoke, or chew gum in public. Each night at sunset, families and friends gathered together to celebrate the breaking of the fast (iftar). The festivities often continued well into the night. In general, things happened more slowly during Ramadan. Many businesses operated on a reduced schedule.

Because of my duty assignments, we soon got military housing on Base. Living on the military base in Morocco was a lot like living in a town back in the States. There was the post office, PX shopping center, doctors, dentists, a church, and other businesses. The base amenities were restricted to resident service members, the U.S. Embassy personnel, and the Royal family of Morocco.

Living on Base, we became even more isolated from the people of our host country. The base was enclosed behind a 20-foot high chain-linked fence and the perimeter was constantly patrolled by armed military...the only interaction with the Moroccan people was with those few who worked on Base: the Fatima who worked as our maid or housekeeper and many unskilled laborers. (Fatima, female name of Arabic origin, commonly used all over the Islamic world. The colloquial use of the term by Americans was in reference to all Moroccan women). For the most part, these workers were interested in learning English and becoming "Westernized."

We were a "Fortress America" plopped down on Moroccan soil. To complete my duties as part of the Navy, I, as was the case with many of our U. S. Navy friends, was not adequately prepared nor interested in learning French or the Arabic language. Such inadequacy in language skills proved later to be a major handicap for me in my interaction with the Moroccan people in general and while working officially with the Moroccan Ministry of Health [45].

The rainy season in Morocco arrived in mid-November, 1962; so, did an increase in the number of patients, both military and their dependents, reporting to hospital complaining of upset stomach and diarrhea. About the same time, I noticed a precipitous increase in the number of stool cultures and an unusual high frequency of enteric pathogens being isolated from these samples. Most preliminary isolates were Shigella species; however, further analysis of some of these isolates by biochemical and serologic methods revealed several Salmonella species as well. (See **Figure #7).**

The Chief and I both recognized the need to track down the source of the contamination. Outside of the military, there were no data on incidence and prevalence of these infectious agents in the indigenous Moroccan families during the early 1960s.

A team was dispatched from U.S. Navy, Preventive Medicine Unit #7, (PMU-7) in Naples, Italy and much to my surprise the team members consisted of two of my former mentors and teachers from Bethesda: Cdr. Arthur King and Chief Joseph Baranski. After a review of our more recent laboratory data, Chief Baranski stated that the investigation must be expanded to include the source of the milk.

The Navy Supply Department had a long-standing contract for purchase of milk and cheese from a firm in nearby Casablanca. The milk products being purchased were not a fresh product, it was from dry powder that was provided by the Navy, and then reconstituted with water, sterilized, and packaged into a cardboard carton at the dairy facility. The containers were then transported weekly by truck back to the Base and placed on shelves for purchase in the Navy Commissary.

Culture results revealed the contamination of the dairy products occurred prior to their arrival on Base. Therefore, the source of contamination had to be either at the dairy or during the transport of the milk to the Base. In either case, the contamination occurred off Base, and finding the source had to be in consultation and with the assistance of the Moroccan Ministry of Health.

In the meantime, and elsewhere in Morocco, the first group of Peace Corps Volunteers (PCVs) had arrived in late January 1963. Group 1 consisted of 53 volunteers who were now ready to serve as language teachers, land surveyors, and water irrigation experts.

Two members of this group, Alex Miller and Duane "Andy" Anderson, who had become ill after being assigned in Boumaine and Midelt in southern Morocco, were now in hospital at the Naval Base in Kenitra. Life in the dessert had not been all that pleasant for them. Instead of being sent back to their irrigation jobs in the South, they were retrained by me to work in the laboratory at the Naval Hospital.

Dr. Melvyn Thorne was the Peace Corps [46] physician assigned to Peace Corps Morocco with practice privileges at the Naval Hospital, and he encouraged the retraining program for the two PCVs. **(Figure #8).**

The diplomatic avenue of approach to the Ministry of Health was accomplished through the able assistance of Dr. Thorne, who in turn introduced us to Dr. Lay Houang, [46] a physician and microbiologist at the Institut d' Hygiene located at 27, Avenue Ibn Battuta in Rabat.

Coincidently, Dr. Houang is the same physician with whom I would later work during an outbreak of bacterial meningitis near Meknes, and while I was with the Peace Corps [46]. He was born in the Belgian Congo to Chinese physician and a French mother. He graduated

185

medical school in France and took subspecialty training in microbiology. He held French and People's Republic of China passports.

It was via Dr. Houang's good offices and laboratories that appointments were made to visit the Dairy in Casablanca, and on the day of inspection, they assisted in the collection of duplicate samples at various intervals throughout the production process, including packaging and storage of the final product before shipment by refrigerated truck to the Base. Collection even included samples of the glue that was being used to seal the sides and the top closure of the wax-paper milk and cheese cartons.

Positive results were isolated in samples from 3 of the 5 aliquots of glue that were used to seal the closure of milk cartons at the Dairy. No other source of contamination was identified. Of considerable interest was the fact the basic nutrients contained in the glue, a liquid adhesive preparation, served as an excellent culture media or medium for, growth and promulgation of the enteric bacteria [47].

The medical team concluded that the Base Supply Officer should look for another source of milk and cheese for sale in the Commissary. Subsequent purchases were made in Rota, Spain and the products were transported to Kenitra weekly via Navy Transport Squadron VR-24 aboard C-130 cargo planes.

Commander. Arthur King and Chief Baranski returned to Naples. Shirley and I visited the Kings' in Naples, climbed the somma-stratovolcano Mount Vesuvius, toured Rome, and took a hydrofoil boat to Capri. Our last visit with the Kings' was in California in the early 1990's, where we had long discussions about some of our experiences in Morocco. I lost track of my dear friend Baranski, but Art later died quietly in Escondido, California, on the 26 February 1999 without fanfare.

In May of 1963, our second son, Dorian Tyler, was born at the U.S. Navy Medical Facility in Kenitra. This was a very happy occasion for the Adams family. Caprice and Darrell were both excited about having a new baby brother. Within the first six-hours of life, it became obvious that Tyler had developed severe jaundice. I soon learned from his laboratory results and his doctor that he was suffering from erythroblastosis fetalis. This event occurred during a time that I now refer to as "the frontier of medicine." Today, erythroblastosis fetalis is not a medical issue in the newborn.

In general, the public health problems in Morocco during the 1960's were similar to those encountered in other developing countries in North Africa at that time. When the French left after 1956 there was little attention given to decaying infrastructure in most cities. Cross-contamination of the drinking water with sewage was a problem, and the consumption of this water frequently caused illness due to the enteric pathogens. Environmental health problems associated with living in the small villages were even greater.

The incidence of infectious diseases in Morocco in the 1960's was not unlike the United States in the mid-1900's. The leading causes of death in both countries were pneumonia, tuberculosis (TB), diarrhea and enteritis; which, together with diphtheria in children, were devastating.

*****

CHAPTER 20

I Slipped Surly Bonds.

$\mathfrak{M}$aynard "Budd" Lang was the third enlisted man who left a life-long notable impression on me. My family sponsored Budd and his family upon their arrival in Morocco in early 1963, as the Kirkpatrick's had done for us a year earlier.

Budd and Cynthia's children shared similar ages with our kids; Jeffery was Darrell's age, Karen was the same age as Caprice, and Mark was Tyler's age. Bud had recently made Chief Hospital Corpsman prior to being transferred to Morocco from Pharmacy School in Portsmouth, Virginia. He was assigned to the Hospital Pharmacy.

While Budd and I were working at the hospital, the children spent their days playing together, and most evenings our two families visited in each other homes and the adults spent time playing pinochle or an occasional game of poker. The neighborhood was typical of most military bases stateside with one exception, we rarely traveled off-base. Shirley and Cynthia spent time shopping in the PX and attending to the needs of their children. Each family household hired a Fatima who lived in the nearby village of Kenitra, for a couple days a week to do some of the housework.

On one occasion, the Lang and Adams families ventured off base and traveled to Ifrane in the Middle Atlas Mountains to go skiing in the Mischliffen ski area. We stayed in the Grande Hotel in Ifrane, a Swiss Alps-like town built by the French in the 1930's during the protectorate era. It is home of Alakhawayn University and a large stone lion statue in the middle of town. Irrespective of what time of day you pass, you will see people lined up to take their picture with it.

It was a Friday evening on 16 December 1963 when Ambassador John Ferguson presented a symbolic key to Moroccan Foreign Minister Reda Guedira, as the U.S. Flag located in front of the Administration Building was lowered for the last time; never to fly again over what was officially a non-existing U.S. Naval Air Facility in Kenitra, Morocco.

The following day, however, "Old Glory" was again saluted, hailed in greeting, and cheered with raised wine glasses and beer cans by many of my buddies and family members as I, with assistance from my friend Budd Lang, ceremoniously raised and tacked another U.S. flag to the West wall inside our Living Quarters aboard the Base.

Also, the three U.S. Air Force SAC Bases at Ben Guerir, Sidi Slimane, and Nouasseur had already left Morocco. And, as noted elsewhere, the United States Navy had agreed to leave Morocco in the fall of 1963.

Being a pilot was something very special to me. I had read somewhere in the 1960's that only about 0.003% of the U.S.

population were pilots. Ever since I was a kid back on the farm, I had always wanted to fly an airplane. That was why I had "hitched" all those rides with my Navy comrades' back at the Naval Air Station in Norfolk. The many times I had spent my lunch-hour "checking-out" a plane with the Overhaul and Repair (O & R) Test Pilots.

On the 3rd of April 1963, I became a full fledge Pilot. I had my "15 minutes of fame" in a Piper Cub. I had made my three takeoffs and landings solo in the old tail-dragger on runway 25 at the Naval Air Facility in Kenitra, Morocco. The three trips around the traffic pattern were uneventful. Soloing was a memorable and historic event for anyone who had long yearned to fly. When the word spread across the airport, many pilots were present for the act of "Running the Gauntlet" or to help me celebrate my "Right of Passage."

This included Navy pilots, as well as private and student pilots who were members of the Aero Club. My instructor, LCdr. Randy Atkinson, was there with scissors in hand and ready to hack off a piece of my shirttail. I had made sure that I wore an old shirt on this particular day, because this scrap of fabric, duly inscribed and autographed with all the important particulars, would be proudly and prominently displayed as a new-pilot's "birth" announcement.

After time, this shred of cloth, which had been hanging with others on the wall of the "Pilot's Briefing Room", came down and was taken home and valued as much as my stiff-paper FAA Airman's Pilot Certificate.

The next day I was up again in the old Piper Cub. It was twilight, and at an altitude of six thousand feet and at a heading of 270 degrees I was playing hide-and-seek with the sun. A slice of its crown was just visible above the horizon from this height. The airplane erased it with a brief, shallow glide, then by climbing caught sight of it again. Down again, another climb, down and up once more--three sunsets and sunrises in barely as many minutes. This was one of those little games that delighted the child in every pilot.

The wind was calm that evening, the engine seemed all in order, and the small plane and I shared an exhilarated mood near the end of a fine summer day. To dissipate what remained of my urge to cavort, I chopped the power off, and pulled the plane's nose up in an exaggerated climb until it stalled. Then I applied full right rudder and held the controls all the way back.

The aircraft bucked once, like a frisky colt let loose, abruptly dropped its nose, kicked its tail up high, and spun toward the ground in the same graceful pattern as a maple leaf descending from a tree. I picked out a landmark and counted the revolutions. One half, one, one and a half, two, two and a half, three--that's enough now, don't overdo it I said to myself. Opposite rudder canceled the turning, a dip of the nose restored lift to the wings, and as the airplane gradually worked out of the spin, moderate G forces pushed me deeper into the seat and a tingling in the stomach offered further confirmation that the machine had responded on cue.

Down some three thousand feet closer to the earth, night was closing in - the favorite moment for those who love to fly. Everything was contentment and serenity here; the plane seemed suspended without motion over a slowly turning planet, alone and yet as one with the cosmos. My position was approaching the town of the Kenitra.

Looking down from that vantage point, I suddenly felt a great surge of euphoria that the Sebou River, lying below was mine. So were the airport, the farms, and the Atlantic Ocean out beyond. Was I high enough to see a thousand miles east and west- that, too, would have all been mine? I had been admitted but only recently into the fraternity of fliers. Eight years had passed since I went flying with my old buddies at Norfolk. Now, at 28 I was legally allowed to set alone in the pilot's seat ... and I loved it!! Within two-weeks of flying the old Piper Cub as a student pilot, I was ready to get checked-out in one of the T-34 aircraft. **Figure #9.** Lou in T-34 at Kenitra, Morocco in 1963

The T-34B, built by Beech Aircraft Corporation, was a two-place tandem trainer equipped with dual flight controls, tricycle landing gear, constant-speed propeller, and duplicate instrumentation in both cockpits. The T-34 was designed to meet all the military requirements of a primary trainer for the Navy and Air Force. It was made available from the Navy for use in the Flying Clubs.

The transition to the T-34 came easy, because I had some time in high-performance aircraft when I was flying in the "right-hand seat" with my Navy chums in Norfolk. I liked the T-34 because it was a giant step-up from the Cub with its Continental six-cylinder engine, and its ability to develop 225 hp. at 2600 rpm at sea level. During training in the T-34, I was impressed with the ease in which one could do acrobatics. I started with some basic flying maneuvers, including "lazy eight's" and the "falling leaf." Soon, under instruction, I was able to master the "spin", "loops" and finally I was able to do "rolls" to the left, to the right, and to stay within 5 degrees of a prescribed heading.

Frequently, my buddy Sam Ayers and I would each take out one of the Flying Clubs T-34s on cross-country trips or to practice "formation flying". We had both received at least 3 hours of instruction with Cdr. Krebs or LCdr. Randy Atkinson, or another one of the Navy pilots who were also members of the Aero Club. Formation flight training was always conducted away from the base in the "practice area" because the Commanding Officer had issued a "Directive" that prohibited such activity within 10 miles of the airport.

One Sunday afternoon, Sam and I decided to take-off and go to the airport at

Tangier and to have lunch. After a complete preflight of both aircraft, we climbed into the cockpit, started our engines and radioed Ground Control for taxi instructions. Since there was little Military Traffic at the airport on Sunday, both planes were cleared to taxi to the Active Runway. Sam was in the lead plane and I followed him down the taxiway to the "run-up area."

After Sam turned his aircraft into the wind and started going through his "Pre-Takeoff Check List," I noticed a puff of blue smoke that came out the exhaust during "run-up. It appeared to happen only after he would throttle-back from the power-check. This did not concern me, because Sam was a good pilot, and if the run-up was not "in the numbers," he would not take-off.

"Kenitra tower, N-92367 ready for take-off," I monitored the instructions over my headset. "N-92367, you are cleared for take-off. Maintain runway heading after take-off until 1500, and then left turnout. Contact Departure Control on 124.55. "Roger, tower...maintain heading till 1500...contact Departure on point five, five," Sam repeated on read-back.

As N-92367 started its take-off roll, I taxied my plane into place and began the "run-up." Everything checked out; I made a clearing turn on the taxiway, and then switched my radio to the tower frequency. But, before I had a chance to say anything, I overheard the controller talking to another plane.

"Navy, Beech 2678 Bravo, you are cleared for a straight-in approach on 25. Contact tower crossing the "Outer Marker" ...Be advised, a T-34 has departed 25...he is now 3 o'clock at 2500 and on a heading of 30 degrees. No other reported traffic." "Roger, tower...report the Outer Marker. Navy, seven-eight Bravo," was the acknowledgement.

"N-93479 hold your position." "Roger, tower. N-93479... hold position," I acknowledge as I glanced to my left looking for the plane on final.

After taking off, I saw Sam's plane make a routine climbing turn to the left and by now he had to be out of the traffic pattern. While waiting for the military plane to land, I again made a "preflight check" of gyros for proper operation, oil pressure and cylinder head temperature gages were in the "green", the mixture lever was at "full rich," the flight controls were free, and the lap-belt and my shoulder harness were snug.

Two or three minutes had passed, and there was still no sight of the twin Beechcraft on final. Then the tower repeated its call for Navy 2678 Bravo over the radio.

"Navy 2678 Bravo...this is Kenitra tower calling... What is your status? Do you copy"? There was no reply. Again, the tower called... still no response. Then, a voice broke-in on the tower frequency, and I recognized Sam's voice.

"Kenitra tower, this is N-92367 and I am about 4 miles east-northeast of the airport and I am afraid that 678 Bravo may have gone down short of the runway? I can see some smoke about two miles off to my left."

"Roger, 367...please standby." "OK, 93479... What are your intentions? Are you ready for takeoff," the controller asks me?

"Roger, tower...93479 is ready for takeoff."

"N-93479, you are cleared for takeoff. Maintain runway heading until 1200 and you are cleared for a left-hand turnout. Stay clear of the traffic pattern, because we have an emergency."

I quickly rolled my plane into take-off position, closed the canopy, lined up with the runway, made a slight adjustment to my gyro to 250 degrees, and slowly advanced the throttle. At about 55 knots, I could feel a good response to elevator control and I then applied slight back-pressure to the stick. With an IAS of 65 knots the aircraft climbed free of the runway.

When the aircraft was airborne, I pulled the landing gear handle to the "Up" position and checked the landing gear lights on the panel. Next, I re-trimmed the aircraft to 90 knots, and made a quick scan of the dials ...2600 rpm and a proper manifold pressure. At 1200 feet of altitude, I moved the stick slightly to the left while applying a little left rudder, keeping the ball and needle centered and in their proper positions.

After turning downwind, I glanced back at the airport, and I could see the fire-trucks and the "Crash-Truck" ambulance, with their emergency lights flashing, racing across the airport to a road that lead off the base and towards the area where black smoke was rising into the air.

Upon clearing the airport control zone, I turned to a heading of 350 degrees to get back on course to Tangier. I had not yet established visual sight with N-92367, but we were in "plane-to-plane" radio contact. After a short exchange of comments regarding "what may have happened with Navy 2678B", my attention returned to the Sectional Map I was using for checking ground reference points during the VFR flight to Tangier.

After 15 minutes into my flight at 4500 feet, the Atlantic Ocean came into view on the left-hand side of the cockpit and the foothills of the Rif Mountains on the right, which provided a beautiful panoramic view of northern Morocco. Within minutes, the Strait of Gibraltar and the blue waters of the Mediterranean Sea came into view over the nose of the aircraft. In addition, I had also made visual contact with N-92367.

After crossing over the little village of Asilah we knew in advance to change radio frequencies in preparation to calling Tangier tower for landing instructions. We both listened to radio communication that was ongoing between a Tangier Tower controller and a pilot of an Air Maroc Caravelle jet airliner. The pilot had just received current altimeter settings and wind direction information, and his clearance to land on runway 28.

"Tangier Tower...this is N-92367 approximately 5 miles South of the airport inbound for a full-stop landing... and I have the numbers."

"N-92367...you are cleared to descend to pattern altitude using runway 28. Be advised there is an Air Maroc "heavy" aircraft on short final ...please, extend your downwind approach to allow the aircraft time to clear the active," came the instructions in perfect English.

After receiving similar instruction from the control tower, I entered the traffic pattern behind N-92367 and proceeded with a routine landing. Ground Control instructed both of us to taxi to the West-end of the flight line and to park near the other small aircraft. This instruction for taxi took the path of our aircraft directly in front of the Terminal building, and nearby the two Air France Caravelle jet aircraft that were parked on the tarmac.

Several General Aviation aircraft were parked in the tie-down area, including a 1949 model 7-AC Aeronca Champ, a British built de Havilland Moth, a Piper J-3 Cub, a 1950 Cessna 170, and other general aviation aircraft.

"You can have Casablanca, Lou, I still think Tangier is the most cosmopolitan city in Morocco," Sam remarked, as we entered the Terminal.

"It certainly has a great history... ruled in turn by Phoenicians, Romans, Vandals, Arabs, Spaniards, and now, the home of many Europeans as well as Moroccans." "I am sure if we got a taxi and went into the city it would give you the opportunity to mingle with many of the European tourist on holiday, Sam...that is, if we had the time," I replied as we made our way into the Pilot's Lounge, just off from the airport restaurant.

Upon entering the restaurant, we both knew that the consumption of any food would be contrary to the established Navy medical policy and the standing recommendation of own Commanding Officer at Kenitra. This restaurant setting, which included a limited menu of taste-satisfying Moroccan cuisine and inviting French pastry, represented a major contrast to the food and life-style available to the military personnel on-base at Kenitra.

Aboard the base, everyone was constantly reminded of the various health hazards associated with eating food "off-base" in the local establishments, and drinking water that was not first boiled to kill the ever-present enteric bacteria. These were the precautions and written instructions that were given to the military regarding proper health standards and sanitation techniques.

They frequently produced such fear as to cause a mental state of a "Fortress

America" aboard the base. Many families were so paranoid about "catching some disease" that they never traveled off the Base during their tour-of-duty in Morocco.

For two of us, we settled for a Coke instead. We paid our 200 francs for the drinks and walked outside the Terminal, passing the many tourists who were waiting to board their commercial plane.

Once seated, Sam asked; "What do think happened to the Navy Beech that was on final approach at Kenitra?"

"Boy, I don't know. From what little the guy in the tower said, it sounds as if he may have lost power, stalled-out or maybe hit a flock of birds. Whatever happened, it must have been sudden, because there was no communication from the pilot about any mechanical problems," I answered.

"Well, from what I could see when I circled over the crash-scene, I don't think anyone could have gotten out. It was burning all around the area. I hope we can find out something when we get back," Sam followed.

"By the way, you see the twin aft-mounted engine configuration on that Air Maroc Caravelle jet? It was put into service on the SE-210 by the French in 1955; and, only United Airlines have started using similarly mounted engines on a plane in the States," I said as we walked to our planes.

Our flight back to Kenitra was uneventful. Later, upon returning to the

Hospital, we did learn that three bodies were recovered from the accident scene. No other information was obtained from any Navy personnel regarding the possible cause of the crash.

Weeks later, the Navy released the following statement regarding the accident:

"The pilot-in-command's improper operation of flight controls during an evasive maneuver to avoid a collision with a flock of birds resulted in the crash. The Accident Board concluded that the pilot had diverted attention from the operation of the aircraft and lost control."

On several occasions while flying one of the T-34s, I tried to imagine what it must have been like to have been one of the first planes off the *USS Ranger* for a bombing run on Port Lyautey during the invasion by Allied Forces in Nov. 1942 [49-52]. From all historical accounts, it had to have been nearly the same easterly heading of 030 degrees the pilots used as they passed over the mouth of the Sebou River inbound to the same base.

Flying at 500-1000-foot altitude, I was sure the pilots passed over the landing craft below as they traveled up the Sebou towards the beachhead for the offloading of troops during the invasion.

On other occasions during my driving tours around the Base, I also tried to visualize what the ground troops might have encountered during their landings.

One of the best accounts of the U.S. military involvement in Morocco during the early phase of WW II was recorded in Pierre Comtois's "First Fire of Operation Torch"[50]. He wrote: "In the crucible of Operation Torch, the men of Sub-Task Force Goalpost received their baptism of fire capturing Port Lyautey in November 1942." [50].

*****

CHAPTER 21

Two Tragedies.

Øctober and November 1963 were painful months for me. Two heartbreaking events occurred in those months, producing lasting memories. The first tragedy involved a young boy who was bitten by his pet dog. The other moment in history that impacted my memory in a significant way was the assassination of President John F. Kennedy.

The first documented case of human rabies in an American stationed in Morocco was encountered in October 1963 near Rabat. The victim was a dependent son of a military family who was stationed with the Embassy group. The child was bitten by a stray mongrel dog that had been "adopted" by the family in early May. Approximately one week following the arrival of the dog, the child received what was thought to be a "playful" bite on the left cheek just below the eye. This calamity bothered me because my own Son, Darrell, was also bitten earlier by an adopted dog.

Only a slight break in the skin was evident, but the father contacted the U.S. Navy Medical Facility in Kenitra for medical advice [57]. Within nine hours, the child was brought to the hospital. The wound was flushed and thoroughly cleansed with a soap solution. To prevent the neutralization of the ammonium compounds, the physician took care to remove all trace of the soap solution before the quaternary ammonium compounds were applied. Because of the circumstances of the bite, anti-rabies therapy was begun immediately.

Following the initial injection of anti-rabies serum, a course of daily injections for 21 days of Duck Embryo Vaccine were administered sub-cutaneous into the child's abdomen, with continued rotation of the injection sites.

The dog was brought to the animal kennels aboard the base at Kenitra for observation. On the fourth day of detention, five days after the patient was bitten, the dog began to exhibit signs of rabies. Eventually, there was paralysis in the dog's hindquarters. The animal was killed, it's head was packed in ice, and the tissue was transported to the Institut de' Pasteur in Casablanca. Confirmation of rabies was made with the observed presence of Negri bodies in the brain tissue.

Five months after the child was bitten, and after having received a full course of anti-rabies therapy, he complained of a sore throat and a mild headache. Otherwise, he remained asymptomatic. On the third day of complaints, the mother was advised to bring the child to the hospital for an examination. The physician admitted the child for observation in view of his having been a victim of a bite from a rabid dog. Upon examination, the physician collected a throat culture and performed a spinal tap. The samples were submitted to the laboratory for bacteriological analysis. After 48-hours, I reported that no bacterial pathogens were isolated.

In the meantime, the child was placed into isolation. His illness progressed to signs of paralysis of the lower extremities, with spasms of the laryngeal and pharyngeal muscles. A periodic state of delirium and convulsions followed. Death occurred four days after admission, as a result of respiratory paralysis. I removed the child's brain, placed the tissue on ice and submitted it for examination of Negri bodies. A positive test result was forthcoming. All health care personnel in attendance of the child, including me, were given post-exposure immunization with the anti-rabies vaccine [57, 58].

Of note is the fact that in start of the 21st Century, the World Health Organization reports that rabies still kills at least 55,000 people worldwide each year, mostly children. In Morocco, human mortality, due to rabies is estimated to be 20 deaths yearly [57] and dog bites are still the main problem. But in the U.S., where pet vaccination and stray-dog-control programs are strong, rabies has a different face: raccoons and skunks are by far the top four-legged viral host. Of interest is the fact that in the U.S., bats have been directly implicated in 20 of 25 human rabies deaths since 1997. (For details see references [57,58]).

October's traumatizing event was bad enough, November's was also very disturbing. On 22 November 1963, President John F. Kennedy, our 35th president was gunned down as his motorcade made its way through downtown Dallas, Texas. My family and I were in Morocco. Do you remember what you were doing the day the President was assassinated? How about when Aldous Huxley died? Or C.S. Lewis? You don't remember? Well, they all three died on 22 November 1963.

More than a half-century later, the world's fascination with JFK hasn't waned. F. Scott Fitzgerald once wrote: "Show me a hero and I will write you a tragedy." Just as we don't get over great losses in our personal lives -- in the sense that the loss is never undone -- so it had been with this young president who captured the imagination of the country for his brief 1,000 days in office. JFK's shocking assassination, dramatically transformed America's domestic and international landscape. At home, his successor, Lyndon Johnson, used the crisis to help pass the long-stalled Civil Rights Act in 1964.

Much has been said about the shock and grief that followed not only in our country but all over the world. Kennedy was the post-war symbol of a revitalized America, a leader determined to move forward at home and abroad on the issues of his day.

It came as a surprise to me that so many Moroccans all over the country felt a sense of personal loss in the death of President Kennedy. It became evident, not only in Morocco but throughout the world, that the impact of John Kennedy had been much greater than Americans had imagined.

The headline in newspapers from around the world, including those in Morocco, told of the assassination. Personnel at the Naval Air Facility in Kenitra, Morocco, first learned of the tragic news by Armed Forces Radio broadcast. The sentiment of most was as expressed in the headlines of the 27 November 1963 European Edition of "The Stars and Stripes" which read: "Grieved Nation Says Farewell to Kennedy."

In a scene, typical of observances throughout the world, mourners in Kenitra paid their last respects to the fallen President. Even the Moroccan people who encountered Americans on the streets Kenitra, Rabat, and in various other cities throughout Morocco expressed their sorrow for the loss of the young President.

Many expressed their concerns regarding who was the responsible party for the killing of the President. Unfortunately, the death of President Kennedy was but a prelude to other killings that plagued our democracy in the early and late 1960's. "Hell no, we won't go!"

These words along with "Hey, Hey LBJ, how many kids have you killed today?" was the rallying cry far and wide. The nation appeared to be splitting into hostile groups.

In April 1968, Martin Luther King, Jr. was murdered in Memphis, and riots followed; in June, Robert Kennedy was killed in Los Angeles; the night he won the Democratic primary.

Protesting students were mowed down at Kent State University in Ohio. College students were protesting the Vietnam War at such noteworthy places as Woodstock and on most campuses; and, the use marijuana and other drugs became more prevalent than ever before.

We continued to demonstrate to the world how we handled our political and social disagreements! Subsequently, and in response to what was occurring, riots broke out in large cities.

If any other event was the defining experience of this generation, it was that war; where more than one-third of age-eligible males served in uniform during that era of the military draft. Whether we fought in the War, or protested against it, the war somehow affected everyone regardless of age.

One day, a son asked his father, "Why is it always the best people who die?" The father answered, "Son, if you are in a meadow, which flowers do you pick? The worst ones or the best?"

"In our sleep, pain which cannot forget falls drop by drop upon the heart until, in our own despair, against our will, comes wisdom through the awful grace of God."

- **Aeschylus**

*****

CHAPTER 22

Travels with Hiram Abiff:

𝕸y journey with Hiram began on 6 October 1964. This was the date when I was initiated as an Entered Apprentice Mason into the Arthur T. Weed Lodge, No. 59, of F. & A. M. in Kenitra, Morocco. At that time, the practice of Freemasonry was illegal in most of the Islamic world; Lebanon and Morocco being the only exceptions.

The Roman Catholic Church had long been an outspoken critic of Freemasonry, first prohibiting Catholics from joining the fraternity in 1738. Since then, the Vatican has made several pronouncements forbidding Catholics from becoming Freemasons under threat of excommunication. After Pope, Clement XII made this pronouncement, the Islamic Theologians were thinking: "If the Pope declares that Freemasons are atheists, there must be some truth in his words.": Since that date, "Freemasonry" in the Ottoman Empire and more recently in other Moslem countries has become synonymous with "atheist."

During dinner that evening prior to the meeting, several Brothers made light hearted comments about riding the proverbial goat and the usual hoax associated with the uninformed; it annoyed me a little, while I understood the sophomoric humor, it was still a situation I was taking very seriously, but again everyone has different perceptions. Also, given the military nature of our lodge it was not unreasonable for there to be this attitude, as when you are new in the military it was customary to make you the brunt of a lot of jokes or ordeals.

As I reflect back over the evening of my initiation over 50 years ago, the one word that keeps jumping around in my mind is "remarkable." As an old farm boy, I was so impressed by the many events of the evening. From the friendliness of the members, to their devotion to the craft; from the seriousness and the awe-inspiring ceremonies; to the skill displayed by the team conducting the degree work. The fact it was also being conducted by my fellow men in uniform certainly made it an extraordinary evening---one I'll not forget.

Our lodge was very casual in appearance and attire, unlike the glitzy, expensive-looking lodges you may see in many pictures from back in the States. The Lodge was inside a WW II Quonset Hut; but it had a close, intimate feel, and, as I said, the ceremony was taken very seriously. What was most amazing about the initiation was that it was "all about me." I was the only candidate that night, so the evening was devoted to my initiation.

The meal, the initiation, the lecture, the social time---all prepared and conducted for me. That busy men would take time out of their lives to prepare and conduct an event spanning several hours specifically for me was truly amazing and humbling. Yet the excitement, joy, and dedication evident in everyone present really spoke volumes to me about their devotion to the fraternity.

After the many questions, I had asked my good friend Budd Lang prior to the meeting, I thought I may have spoiled some of the evening, but it turns out that I simply didn't know what to expect. The prevailing mantra during the evening was, "Everyone here went through the exact same thing." By those remarks, I wasn't sure to be comforted or intimidated!

The whole evening was at the same time solemn, exciting, humorous, friendly, unnerving, intriguing, educational, and yet informative. After it was over, I was asked what I thought of the evening by the Worshipful Master. I said I was impressed by the ceremony; and that it was not what I had expected. But, I could not wait to go through the remaining two degrees.

So, I was now an Entered Apprentice Mason. But like so many of the steps in life's journeys, this was just the beginning. It was now time to go to work. My proficiency work consisted of lots of memorization. The Obligation, lots of questions, and knowledge of the working tools were all essential things that I had to memorize.

I was told repeatedly by Budd Lang, my mentor that learning the Ritual was very manageable, and it would be exciting to learn. I looked forward to our next meeting and appreciated his assistance in helping me decipher the coded word.

Although, as I later learned, we only receive the fullness of truth in the Third Degree, while the Second Degree was a form of "Purgatory" where we spend our lives: working, hoping, shoring up our weaknesses, but not completely, and asking the many questions which, we hope, would lead us to the truth.

The Sublime or Master Mason Degree was where Masonry endeavored to take me; and, the Initiatory Degree was where my journey began. In any event, on 1 December 1964, I completed the last leg of my journey with the help and guidance of the Senior Deacon, Brother Budd Lang.

During the ceremony when being lead around blindfolded, I could sense a difference in the tone of the ritual; it was much more solemn. The obligation represented the majority of the first part of the degree, wherein I was asked if I would be willing to give up my safety and comfort to aid a brother, without any reference to race, color, creed or religion; something that I took then and still take very seriously today!

At a later point in the ceremony I was directed to an Alter to pray; at that moment, everything got very personal and the ritual took on an entirely different meaning. Although representing a setting for one's mind, the allegorical scenes that followed depicted meaningful stories that are applicable to the larger issues that confront mankind today. As explained in the lecture that followed the degree work, the moral of the story was a lesson in fidelity to one's word, and an important reference to the brevity of life.

Upon my return to the States in 1966, I petitioned Scioto #6, in Chillicothe, Ohio, one of the oldest Masonic Lodges in Ohio; also, having an interesting history. Over 211 years ago, on 10 September 1805, the Grand Lodge of Massachusetts received a petition requesting a Charter for this lodge in the town of Chillicothe, and after being granted unanimously it was named Lodge #2. The first meeting occurred 22 November that year in the home of Thomas Needham, a tavern keeper. It was later assigned the title of Scioto #6 under the auspicious of the Grand Lodge of Ohio.

It was here I achieved a greater appreciation of the fraternity and sought to expand my knowledge of Masonry. I became a member of the Scottish Rite and York Rite. I learned that Scottish Rite sought to strengthen the community and each man should act in civil life according to his individual judgment and the dictates of his conscience.

York Rite is a term most often used in the United States of America to refer to a collection of Masonic degrees that, in most other countries, are conferred separately. It is here I learned that a Master Mason may proceed to supplement and amplify the Blue Lodge degrees, thereby affording historical background on the work and meaning of Freemasonry.

In 1968, after taking a faculty position at the U. of Cincinnati, I joined

McMakin Lodge #120 in Mount Healthy, a small town near Cincinnati. As they got older, both Darrell and Tyler displayed an interest in DeMolay and when they joined I became a "DeMolay Dad". Having both sons in DeMolay was one of the proudest moments of my life because the Order of DeMolay uses ritual and symbolism to engrave wise and serious truths on the hearts and minds of young men. The words were crafted like a fine painting, all working in concert to impress the ideals of fidelity and toleration in a manner solemn and yet, understandable, to young men.

Periodically, I have had an opportunity to visit Chandlersville Lodge #858 near River, Kentucky where my Uncles and Cousins attended. Figure #10 shows (l to r) Louis Adams, Cecil Castle, and Paul Eugene Daniels. Both Cecil and Paul are members of this Masonic Lodge.

At the time of this writing, I had been a Mason for over fifty years and was serving as Secretary of Columbia Lodge #44 in Miamitown, a small town some 20 miles west of Cincinnati. Members of the lodge were a friendly lot, most of whom were residents of the town, small villages nearby or living in a rural area within a 10-25-mile radius.

This Lodge has had a long and interesting history: Chartered in 1817, the first Worshipful Master was Othneil Looker, the fifth governor of Ohio. Looker, born in New York, served in the New Jersey militia in 1776, and after receiving a land grant in Ohio for his time in war services eventually settled in what is now Harrison, Ohio. He was badly defeated in 1814 as governor of Ohio by Thomas Worthington from Chillicothe, OH.

Since 2015, not unlike other fraternal originations, poor attendance, lack of recruitment of new members, and dire financial straits, forced a merger of Columbia with Nova Caesearea Harmony Lodge No. 2 F. & A. M. This fact has not prevented several of the living past masters of Columbia Lodge to tell some colorful stories of their past: "How things use to be when the lodge was overflowing with members in attendance of their Stated Meetings!"

One such 92-year old Past Master, John Nullmeier, reiterated a story of a time back when a couple of bandits from Morgan's Raiders attempted to break into and steal items from the Lodge when they pass through Miamitown in early July 1863 and on their way through such more northern communities and avoiding the more heavily armed Cincinnati and Camp Dennison.

Our current commemoration of the Civil War Sesquicentennial during these early years of the 21st century will, hopefully, provide an excellent opportunity to educate young and old alike about that dark national crisis that affected all Americans, rich and poor, free and slave, and continues to influence our culture.

Few young are aware and only limited number of elderly remember the fact that the Civil War resulted in as many

217

American deaths as all of the other subsequent wars combined. Over six hundred and twenty thousand military men from both sides lost their lives, along with the tens of thousands of civilians who perished during those four years. Maybe somewhere along the Trail young and old alike will learn a little history?

An interesting sideline that is a part of history is the Battle of Buffington Island 19 July 1863. This was the largest battle in Ohio during that war, and it contributed to the capture of Morgan by Brig. General Edward Henry Hobson who is a distant relative of my wife, Shirley. He was an officer in the United States Army in the Mexican-American War and the Civil War. Morgan and most of his officers who were confined to a jail in Columbus, Ohio, but later escape and return safely to Kentucky.

A short time after I left the Navy, Budd Lang served with Special Forces in Vietnam and Cambodia. During duty, there he was exposed to an herbicide(s) that was then only referred to as "Agent Orange." An unintended byproduct of Agent Orange, was the highly toxic chemical dioxin.

Later we learned that he had joined other returned Veterans associations who were having similar medical problems in an effort to call attention to the possible exposure to some chemical toxins. For years, our government's rebuttal was that there was no direct link or cause and effect to such exposure.

Some 20 years later the Institute of Medicine reported "evidence of an association" between exposure to Agent Orange even though side-effects of dioxin have long been linked to several forms of cancer, adult-onset diabetes, ischemic heart disease, Parkinson's disease, hairy-cell leukemia, and birth defects. Today, the VA pays disability compensation for many of these known conditions or diseases presumed to have been caused by exposure to these defoliants.

Budd died 23 Oct 1998 in Virginia Beach, Virginia. Death came after a breakup of his marriage, much pain and suffering by his children, and his long-term physical and mental side-effects from exposure to Agent Orange while serving our country. Admission of guilt or acknowledgement came too late for Budd and the over 200,000 others who were exposed as part of some 2.6 million men who served on the ground in Vietnam...say nothing of their military family members who were also affected.

*****

CHAPTER 23

The Final Chapter

The signature of Captain William Parrish, USN, and the commander of the American-run communication bases centered at Kenitra, 25 miles north of the Moroccan capital of Rabat, formally handed over to the Moroccan Government all that remained of the multimillion dollar installations. (See Addendum E).

They were the last in a succession of tens of thousands of American troops who had served in Morocco since General George S. Patton's GIs stormed ashore on 8 November 1942, and captured Kenitra - then named Port Lyautey - from the forces of Vichy France in a 3-day battle that cost the lives of 567 Americans [11,49-55].

Greatly expanded and modernized by the United States over the years, the bases at Kenitra, and neighboring Sidi Yahia and Sidi Bouknadel were placed under nominal Moroccan command during my duty there in 1960's to counter communist and Third World criticism; similar to the condemnation raised against the former U.S. military facilities in Libya and Ethiopia. Those facilities were abandoned also after new governments came to power in those countries.

In fact, at the height of their importance in the 1950s and early 1960s, the bases in Morocco served as a major U.S. arms depot, Naval Air Station, staging point and platform for U.S. Navy anti-submarine and electronic counter-measures, and provided transport squadrons in support of our 6th Fleet Operations. (See Addendum F).

In conclusion, the United States and Morocco have had a treaty of friendship since 1787, the longest unbroken peace agreement the U.S. has maintained with any country in the world [55]. Since 1950, Morocco has received more U.S. aid than any other Arab or African country, except for Egypt. Indeed, since the beginning of the war over Western Sahara, Morocco has received more than one-fifth of all U.S. aid to the continent, totaling more than $1 billion in military assistance and $1.3 billion in economic aid [55].

In return, Morocco has remained one of Washington's closest strategic allies in either Africa or the Arab world, particularly during the early years of the Reagan administration. Morocco continues to allow the U.S. Navy access to its port facilities and grants the U.S. Air Force landing, refueling, over flight rights, and an emergency landing field near Marrakesh for use following Shuttle launching by NASA. There remains a close cooperation in intelligence and communications.

Despite a history of close relations with Iraq, Morocco sent forces to Saudi Arabia in 1990 to support the U.S.-led war effort to liberate Kuwait. In addition, the United States and Morocco have cooperated militarily in supporting pro-Western regimes in Africa, and Morocco has engaged in destabilizing efforts against radical African states, with apparent close collaboration with the U.S. Central Intelligence Agency (CIA).

In fact, as a testament of their loyalty to duty in Morocco, former military and civilian personnel assigned there over those years have become life members of the Moroccan Reunion Association which meets yearly in select cities throughout the U.S to exchange war stories and share fond memories.

The phasing out of U.S. Military in Morocco during the 1960's does not imply any loss of interest in the area. Rather to the contrary, we maintained and enlarged our presence with more suffocated spy ships in the Sixth Fleet in the Mediterranean [55].

Not only was the U.S. Military presence being reduced in Morocco, my enlistment in the U.S. Navy was coming to a close. I was at a critical juncture in my life regarding my career and some major decisions had to be made soon. The Navy had refused my request to attend Chemistry School, so Shirley and I had decided that I should get out and go college.

In retrospect, given my acquisition of knowledge and practical experience in Morocco, I now question the value of the withdrawal of Americans into a state of "Fortress America" behind the fenced-in walls of the base at Kenitra which was purported to be for our security, protection, and disease prevention.

When public services and even local government aboard the base were under U.S. Military rule, when the community of responsibility stopped at the guarded gates, what happened to idea of real culture exchange, the potential for social interaction, and the planting of the seed for political democracy? Can any nation fulfill its social contract in the absence of social contact?

"Travel is fatal to prejudice, bigotry, and narrow-mindedness, and many of our people need it sorely on these accounts" [1].

When one speaks of the Arab world, historians know this includes a vast geographic area, comprising many different countries in Asia and Africa. The contemporary world owes much of its progress in all fields of human intellectual activity, including medicine, to Arabic culture, especially the early advancements made in the 8th to 13th centuries- a period known as the "Golden Age of Arabic-Islamic Science."

Who knows what will eventually shake-out from the "Arab Spring," only time will tell? One thing is for sure it is for the local citizens to decide their own future. In the end, it may well become known as the Western World's "Winter of Discontent."

*****

CHAPTER 24

Out of the U.S. Navy.

Since my tour of duty in Morocco ended and I was getting out of the Navy, Dr. Melvyn Thorne, the Peace Corps physician in Morocco asked if I would be willing to meet with him to discuss an idea he had for a new Peace Corps program proposal for Morocco. We met with Drs. Houang, Sinclair-Loutit, Director of World Health Origination/Morocco (WHO), and Dr. Larbi Chraibi, the Minster of Health for Morocco. The meeting was held in Dr. Houang's office at the Institut de' Hygiene in Rabat.

After introductions, Dr. Sinclair-Loutit was asked to give a brief overview of public health problems in the rural areas in the country. Dr Chraibi acknowledged that health care services in Morocco were extremely poor, with basic and outdated equipment, a small number of health facilities and fewer than 1,000 doctors for the entire population. Some health centers had closed due to lack of staff, equipment or medical supplies. In closing, he said that the immediate need was for laboratory assistants to work in the hospitals and clinics.

At this point, Dr. Thorne presented his proposal that would help alleviate the problem in the short-term using Peace Corps Volunteers. We had a frank discussion about the limited, on-the-job laboratory training program I help provide the two PCVs, Alex and Andy, during their hospital convalesce at the Medical Facility in Kenitra some months earlier.

According to Dr. Taza, the Laboratory Director of Avaincence Hospital in Rabat, where the two PCVs were working, he was very pleased with their knowledge and laboratory performance. Dr. Thorne added that similarly trained Lab Techs may be of help in other hospitals throughout Morocco. This critique was well received by the Minister of Health.

Dr. Chraibi asked if I would consider applying for the position as the "Laboratory Program Director" for the Peace Corps in Morocco. Since my family and I had lived in Morocco for over two years, and because I had already established a good, professional working relationship with Dr. Houang Lay at the Institut de' Hygiene, the Minster stated I should be offered the job. Dr. Thorne stated that he felt I would certainly be a strong candidate for the position.

The Institut de' Hygiene in Morocco, which was similar to our National Institute of Health (NIH) and Communicable Disease Center (CDC) in Atlanta, Georgia, was inaugurated on 30 December 1930 in Rabat by Professor Leon Bernard, Chairman of the Health Council of Australia, chaired by Mr. Lucien Saint, Resident General of France in Morocco to address problems of hygiene and epidemiology of communicable diseases in Morocco and spread the basics of hygiene and prophylaxis to protect the health of the population. In 1963, Dr. Houang became the Director of the Department of Bacteriology within this institution.

My application process included additional interviews with the in-country Director of the Peace Corps, Dr. Thomas Carter, and one of his Associate Directors, Mr. Paul Ator in their offices in Rabat. The meeting took place on a Saturday afternoon, one week prior to my departure for the States, and my release from the U.S. Navy. There was no assessment or feedback provided me after the meeting.

My family and I left Morocco and returned to Ohio via Philadelphia, Pennsylvania. In Philadelphia, I was released from the regular U.S. Navy after 11 years and four months of active service.

We first visited Shirley's parents near Fort Meade and tried to assimilate into a somewhat normal routine as a family, even though the five-additional people in the household was somewhat a burden on her parents.

In Ohio, we moved into the old farmhouse I had help build years earlier on Walnut Creek Road. Mom and Dad had relocated into their new house on Hough Road and I began to do some farm-work.

Unsure I would be selected for the job with the Peace Corps, I decided to explore the possibility of getting a job to support my family and to enrolling in college at the Ohio University.

*****

Photographs & Captions

Figure #1. Pearlie Jane Adams and family at Logan Elm in 1970. (l-r) Jewel, Lucyibelle, Earsel, Virginia Mae, Gladys, Jake, Eugene, Pearlie Jane, Opal, and Madeline.

Figure #2. Earsel Adams Family in the 1980's. (l-r) Lennard, Ruth Ann, David, Earsel, Bernard Ray, Iuka, Ed, Betty Jane, Bert, and Lou.

Figure #3. *U.S.S. Tarawa (CVS-40).*

Figure #4. Adams Brothers aboard the
Tarawa. Lou (r to l) offers support while
Ed receives a shot from Bert.

Figure #5. Bert (on left) extending a welcome to his brother David Larry Adams aboard USS Skylark.

Figure #6. D.K. Lawless and Margaret in 1948.

Figure #7. Lou in Lab at Kenitra, Morocco Naval Hospital in 1963.

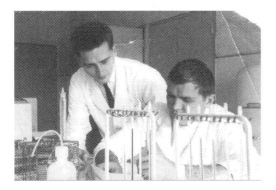

Figure #8. PCVs Alex Miller and Dawne "Andy" Anderson in Dr. Taza's lab in Rabat, Morocco

Figure #9. Lou in T-34 at Kenitra, Morocco in 1963.

Figure #10. Masonic Lodge Brothers. (l to r) Lou Adams, Cecile Castle, and Paul Daniels.

Addendum A,

Some may say we have made progress in medical care since my grandmother was growing up in the late 1800's. Unfortunately, persons suffering from a serious, chronic illness such as arthritis who have not found sustained relief from pain may resort to taking supplements along with their prescribed medications. They do so without any appreciation of a possible synergistic interaction of such combinations or may be unaware of potential latent side-effects from taking such compounds. Unappreciated, is the fact that some rheumatic diseases will frequently wax and wane and the patient may think the new concoction is producing the desired pain relief.

Although some folk medicine is still in use today, the major reasons for the extended earlier practices can be summarized simplistically as cultural and socioeconomic differences. The economic differences began to disappear when President Johnson's "War on Poverty" programs of the mid-1960's went into effect, but it did little to change cultural beliefs.

There were many contributing factors as to why conventional medical care was not sought and used by folks in rural America during these times. Cavender [13] and others [14,16] have provided a plethora of data suggesting a "cause and effect" that will keep anthropologists, health planners, and academicians employed for many years.

However, I think the so called Magico-religious folk medical belief system is still in play. The relationship between spirituality and medicine has been present in many cultures [9,15,16]. Despite their differences in history, society, economy, and culture, the Appalachian folk shared a common belief that spirituality and religion played an important role in the healing process of diseases [9,15,16].

On the other side of the coin, recent data reveal it's not just the "Over-the-Counter" products. There may be a much greater problem-over medicated Americans? The basic question: Who is to blame and are Americans a nation of pill poppers? In his book entitled "Overdosed America," Abramson [17] concluded we have a serious problem. Not only are people now taking more medications than ever, but doctors are prescribing more than ever, too. Prescriptions for pain, Arthritis, upper respiratory problems, and diabetes dominate the list.

An increase percentage of U.S. health-care costs is being spent on prescription drugs and the amount has doubled since 1970's. The main offenders are the over-prescribing and use of antibiotics. Only about 10% of sore throat cases in adults are due to strep throat, but doctors admit to prescribing antibiotics in 60% of patients with sore throats that they see [17]. Because of the over-prescribing of antibiotics, the bacteria that these drugs are meant to kill have become resistant to them, creating "superbugs" [18].

We are a nation of pill poppers. Nearly 13 prescriptions were written per man, woman, and child last year. We're one of only two countries in the world who allow direct-to-consumer drug advertising; the other country is New Zealand. Their Parliament has recently decided to review that policy and may withdraw from using that advertising practice.

How many times have you heard: "Ask your doctor if drug 'xyz'," can be prescribed for your ailment?" Nightly news programs contain from five to seven prescription drug commercials. Cost of advertisements is one reason prescription drug cost have slowly grown to be the third highest medical component of health care.

Is it to anyone's surprise that recent data suggests the deaths from illicit drugs and misuse and overdose of prescription drugs surpasses motor vehicle deaths in Appalachia?

Keven Williamson [19] summed it up best in his article entitled: "The White Ghetto. In Appalachia, the country is beautiful and the society is broken." It reads in part: "Thinking about the future in Appalachia and its bleak prospects is not much fun at all [9,19]. You have the pills and the dope, the morning beers, the endless scratch-off lotto cards, healing meetings up on the hill, the federally funded ritual of trading cases of food-stamp Pepsi for packs of cigarettes and good old hard currency, tall piles of gas-station nachos, the occasional blast of meth, Narcotics Anonymous meetings, petty crime, the draw, the recreational making and surgical unmaking of teenaged mothers, and death."

The business of America, is big business! Hey, Big Pharma is big business. What's wrong with America is what's wrong with Big Pharma. And what's wrong with Big Pharma is what's wrong with America's Health Care System. The **industry** (17) demonstrates its power, political might and social influence over this nation's government and agencies, its health care systems, its doctors and hospitals, as well as its psyche, all at the expense of the American people.

*****

Addendum B

From: Carlo Iachini
Sent: Monday, September 12, 2016 3:28 PM
To: theoldprofessor@gmail.com
Subject: VP- 56 plane crash

Dear Louis, I was not there the night of the plane hitting the seawall. I flew with some of the survivors and learned that the pilot and co-pilot mistook the runway lights for the sealane lights. The bay was calm and the plane had a difficult time breaking suction and started proposing and in the confusion, they saw the runway lights and headed for them. That was quite a trick to get between the seawall and boat house and line up with the runway. When they noticed their error, one officer chopped the throttles and the other slammed them forward which caused the plane to almost miss the sea wall but caught the hull just below the flight deck and sheared it off. The men they lost were in their respective take-off and landing stations. Down and aft of the port entry door. The tail section was tossed down the runway, almost intact. The hull, with its rubber bladder tanks full of fuel landed on top of the crew members and more than likely drowned them. The crew members were comprised of two ordnance men, two mechanics, and four techs, plus pilot, co-pilot and navigator. A tech or radioman normally sat the electrical panel, a mechanic stood on the steps leading up into the cockpit monitoring fuel controls while the navigator sat at the plotting table and the remainder of the crew was down and aft. I heard rumors to the effect that the Breezy Point toward was manned but the people were not responding to the plane's questions and directions. Some assume they may have been preoccupied with other interests. Hope you can use what I have provided. Have a good day. Bye for now, Ike

Addendum C

Corpsmen ([75]) were first sent into battle during the Spanish American War in 1898 with the Marine Corps at Guantanamo Bay, Cuba. Later during WW I, 348 Corpsmen were stationed with the Marines; and 17 were Killed in Action (KIA), and two received the Medal of Honor. One of the well-known stories out of WW II included the fact that a Corpsman with the Marines (FMF duty) by the name of John Bradley helped raise the flag on Iwo Jima.

A second, and one of the greatest stories for our time, was the history of George E. Wahlen who was also a Hospital Corpsman at the same battle for Iwo Jima, the bloodiest battle of the modern era. Risking his life to save others, Wahlen was injured three times before being carried off the battlefield. For his actions, he was awarded the Medal of Honor-- our nation's highest military honor.

The third story that had wide circulation was about "Johnny "Bryson Lipes, a First-Class Corpsman aboard the submarine *U.S.S. Seadragon*, (SS-194), who had removed an appendix from a shipmate while submerged under the Pacific Ocean during that same War.

He was the first of three successful surgeries by submarine Corpsmen during that war; but, Lipes was ostracized by Navy Medical Corps physicians. It was said they were angered by his actions, even though he had been obeying his captain's orders. There also was talk of a court-martial by the outraged U.S. Surgeon General, who was forced later to set protocols for appendectomies on submarines.

Lipes later got a Commission in the Medical Service Corps (MSC), retired as a lieutenant commander, and died 17 April 2005 in a hospital in New Bern, N.C at age 84 after an extended battle with pancreatic cancer.

As a matter of general interest, of the 1,102 Navy personnel killed in action (KIA) during Viet Nam, 776 (70%) were Hospital Corpsmen or "Medics" serving with the Marines. To date there have been 20 U.S. Navy Ships named in honor of fallen Hospital Corpsmen. They include the following:

1). *USS Benfold* (DDG-65) was named for *Edward Clyde Benfold* who was killed on 5 Sept 1952, while serving with the 1st Marine Division in the Korean War.

2). *USS Caron* (DD-970) was a destroyer that was named after *Wayne Maurice Caron* who was killed on 28 July 1968 while serving with the Marines in Vietnam. He was posthumously awarded the Medal of Honor.

3). *USS De Wert* (FFG-45) was named for *Richard David De Wert* who was killed on 5 April 1951 while serving with the 7th Marines during the Korean War. He was posthumously awarded the Medal of Honor.

4). *USS Durant* (DER-389) was named for *Kenneth W. Durant* who was killed 3 Nov 1942 while serving with the Marines on Guadalcanal, Solomon Islands.

5). *USS Frament* (APD-77) was named after *Paul Stanley Frament* who was killed on 19 Nov 1942 on Guadalcanal in the Solomon Islands while serving with the U.S. Marines. He was posthumously awarded the Silver Star.

6). *USS Halyburton* (FFG-40). This ship was named for *William David Halbburton, Jr.* who died 10 May 1945 while serving with the U.S. Marines during battle on Okinawa. He was posthumously awarded the Medal of Honor.

7). *USS Francis Hammond* (FF-1067) was named for *Francis Colton Hammond* who died in Korea on 26 Mar 1953 while serving with U.S. Marines. He received Medal of Honor.

8). *USS Jobb* (DE-707) was named after *Richard Patrick Jobb* who was killed on 26 Jan 1943 at Guadalcanal. He was posthumously awarded the Silver Star.

9). *USS Daniel A. Joy* (DE-585) was named for *Daniel Albert Joy* who was killed in action on 5 Oct 1945 on Guadalcanal with the U.S. Marines.

10. *USS Lester* (DE-1022) named after *Fred Faukner Lester* who was serving with the U.S. Marines on Okinawa on 8 June 1945 during WW II.

11). *USS Liddle* (DE-206) was named after *William Porter Liddle* who was killed on 19 Aug 1942 while serving with 1st Marine Division on Guadalcanal.

12). *USS Litchfield* (AG-95) named for *John Litchfield* who was killed on 15 Sept 1918 while serving with the USMC near Thiacourt, France during World War I. He was posthumously awarded the Distinguished Service Cross.

13). *USS Thaddeus Parker* (DE-369) was named in honor of *Thaddeus Parker* who was killed 20 July 1943 while serving with the U.S. Marines on Guadalcanal. He was posthumously awarded the Purple Heart, Navy Cross, and Silver Star.

14*). USS David R. Ray* (DD-971) was named for *David Robert Ray* who was killed on 19 Mar 1969 while serving with the U.S. Marines during the Vietnam War. He was posthumously awarded the Purple Heart and Medal of Honor.

15). *USS Henry W. Tucker* (DD-875) was named in honor of *Henry W. Tucker* who was killed during the Battle of the Coral Sea on 7 May 1942 in WW II. He was posthumously awarded the Navy Cross.

16). *USS Walter C. Wann* (DE-412) was named in honor of *Walter Carl Wann* who was killed while assigned with the U.S. Marines on the Solomon Islands on 4 Nov 1942 during WW II. He was posthumously awarded the Silver Star.

17). *USS Jack Williams* (FFG-24) was named in honor of *Jack Williams* who was killed on 3 Mar 1945 while with the Marines in the Battle of Iwo Jima during WW II. He was posthumously awarded the Medal of Honor.

18). *USS John Willis* (DE-1027) was named after *John Harlan Willis* who was killed on 28 Feb 1945 while with the U.S. Marines on Iwo Jima. He was later awarded the Medal of Honor posthumously.

19). *USS Don O. Woods* (APD-118) was named to honor *Don Otis Woods* who died from wounds received on 8 Aug 1942 while serving with the U.S. marines on the Solomon Islands during WW II. He was posthumously awarded the Silver Star.

20). *USS Valdez* (FF-1096) was named for *Phil Isadore Valdez* who was killed in action on 29 Jan 1967 while serving with the U.S. Marines in the Republic of Vietnam. He was posthumously awarded the Navy Cross.

As a footnote: "Today, while doctors have borne some of the adversity of our most recent wars in Iraq and Afghanistan, where burns, amputations and blast wounds from roadside bombs have shattered so many lives, but by far it is still the Hospital Corpsmen who are bearing the brunt of seeing the killing and maiming of bodies first because they are on the front lines with their Marine units. At least 220 "medics" have been killed so far in these two wars."

Those who perform these tasks do not consider themselves a hero, they are just doing their duty!

Addendum D

After living, working, and conducting some study, I have acquired a greater appreciation for the mutual relationships between Morocco and the United States. In the early 1960s, Morocco was one of 54 countries inside the Africa containing more than 925 million inhabitants who spoke over 1,000 dialects or languages. That was the general part of the world where the Pharaohs once ruled, and where history reminds us that most of the available scientific evidence suggests that Africa may have been the continent in which all human life began [53].

Nonetheless, as Americans we generally simplify and observe Moroccan history in three (3) broad categories:

I The Early Years:

An indigenous people known as Berbers [61] who were already well established across North Africa when the Phoenicians made their first incursions into the continent around 1200 B.C.E. [62].

The Phoenicians were essentially a maritime people who established trading posts and fish-salting factories along the Mediterranean and this north coast of Africa; and, traces of their occupation have been found in Tangier, Melilla, Chellah, Rabat, and near the town of Tetouan, Morocco. History also suggest that they were not interested in conquering or colonizing as were the French, Spanish, and British in later years, and they paid little attention to the primitive Berber tribes and their poor agricultural land within the interior of Morocco.

By the beginning of the 5th century BCE, the Roman Empire had conquered most of the old Phoenician colonies and they had taken control of the entire Mediterranean coastline from what is now modern Morocco and eastward to the borders of Egypt. Also, most Americans have to be reminded that Rabat is only 2093 Nautical miles west of Jerusalem, an area that is frequently referred to as the "Cradle and Crucible" of modern Christian religion. In Jerusalem and on the lands nearby are the stony hills where we were told Jesus walked, taught, performed healings, and died on a wooden cross.

Next 400 years formed Morocco 's "Dark Age" and very little detail is known about that period; although, the Vandals who we're sweeping through Spain may have touched the northern tip of Morocco on their way eastwards to Carthage, but I was unable to find and historical records as to the length of their stay.

"Moors," a rather outdated word now, and one with a distinct pejorative image, was popular in European languages in the late medieval and early modern time periods. It is no coincidence that most eighteenth-century writers who referred to the land that was inhabited by the Moors as Mauritania and Morocco or as the "Land of the Blacks." They were considered by some as being enemies of Christian Europe, and believed all to be black as presented in Shakespeare's Othello.

The Berbers who were in the mountains and the desert during that early history continued life much as before. The term Berber [59] remains largely a linguistic one, describing people who speak one of several dialects. Some of Morocco's Jewish communities were also established during what was called the Phoenician period and later during the Spanish Inquisition when many Berbers converted to Judaism before the Arab Conquest.

The Arabic influence was a cultural one, not radicalism. Islam was at the same time a religion, a government, and a code of ethical conduct. The Arab-Berber dualism in Morocco has been best described by Blair [53].

The city of Meknes, often referred to as the "Versailles of Morocco," is a Name that resonates throughout early Moroccan history, which was lavishly expressed as the palace built by Sultan Moulay Ismail (1672-1727) [62,63,65].

Nearby, are the Roman ruins in Volubilis, a Roman settlement on what may have been a Carthaginian city, dating from the third century BCE. The city of Moulay Idriss is home to the shrine of the founder of Morocco's first imperial dynasty. (See picture on back cover).

Although Morocco was not part of the Ottoman Empire, Moroccan pirates [62] held their activities in both the Mediterranean Sea and southward alone the Atlantic Ocean. They used two main ports as their bases; one was Tetouan in the north and the other was Salé, near

Rabat. From these two ports, the pirates roamed the seas bringing back loot and slaves from as far away as the shores of the Americas [62-68].

The fictional character Robinson Crusoe in Daniel Defoe's novel by the same name sailed from this coast in the Atlantic Ocean and into the *Bou Regreg River* which still separates the cities of Rabat and Salé [68].

The remains of Volubilis, near the cities of Moulay Idriss and Fes are enduring monuments that pay tribute to the astonishing reach of the Roman Empire. Indeed, in northwest Africa these ruins mark Rome's farthest frontier [46].

After our independence from England in 1776, Morocco was the first nation to recognize the sovereignty of the United States in 1778 [65,66,69]. Five years later, the United States made peace with and was recognized by Great Britain; and, in 1784 the first American ship was captured by pirates from Morocco. After six months of negotiation, a treaty of friendship between the U.S. and Morocco was signed, $60,000 cash was paid to get the ship released, and trade began.

Not long thereafter, one of the first of several "Private Agreements," or as I prefer to call them "Diplomatic Blunders," was made among the United Kingdom, Italy and France in 1904. Herein a decision was made, without consulting the Sultan, which divided the Maghreb into spheres of influence, with France and Spain given Morocco [55,66,69].

Later, the Treaty of Fez was signed by the Sultan on 30 March 1912; this act officially gave up control of Morocco to the French, making the country a protectorate. Spain also gained some land in the northern section which became known as Spanish Morocco. By the agreement signed with France and Spain, Spain assumed a protectorate over Tangier, the Rif Mountains, and Ifni, a small area of land on the Atlantic coast in the southwest, and France became the protectorate of the remainder. Yusef ruled the French Protectorate from 1912 until his death in 1927. This treaty was perceived as a betrayal by most Moroccans [55,59,65,66,69].

Political and military events such as these have occurred in Morocco since the dawn of the 20th Century and critical reviews have been presented by historians and functionaries in the traditional, bureaucratic or "official" format [55,66,69].

However, recently Blair, Murphy and Terkel have all presented these historical events in a more contemporary and progressive manner which appear more rational and easy to appreciate and sanction [11, 55, 69]. An example being what happened after the *Treaty of Fes* was signed and France began to rule most of Morocco [55,65].

Louis Hubert Gonzalve Lyautey was appointed High Commissioner and Resident General in French Morocco on 27 April 1912. His policy was "divide and rule" both politically and militarily. He supported the King publicly and always deferred to him socially, but he surreptitiously utilized political and economic opposition to the sultan's government along racial lines-- Berber against Arab [55].

To secure Berber cooperation, Lyautey gave up the less useful parts of Morocco, the mountains and the desert, to the Grand Caids and local village councils, who had paid only nominal homage to the sultan. Overall, Lyautey promoted a class system in Morocco; this was most evident later in the education system [55, 63]. A review of other important writings often failed to present these critical details [52, 55,63,69].

II. Pre-WW II History of Morocco:

"Why were the German and Italian Armies in North Africa prior to World War II?" "Have you ever asked anyone this question?"

Although the answer may not have been emphasized during your high school and college history lectures, there were some major economic factors involved in the decision-making process by Axis powers and the Allies prior to the start of World War II.

Part of the answer, as we all learned, included the fact World War I had left a tremendous political dislocation in Europe. These displacements laid the groundwork for the collapse of democratic institutions on the continent and set the stage for a German power struggle. The already fragile democratic regime in

Germany was further weakened by the worldwide depression that began in 1929.

This environment permitted Adolf Hitler to bring to power the Nazi Party in 1933, a mass movement that was virulently nationalistic, anti-democratic, and anti-Semitic. He ended parliamentary government, assumed dictatorial powers, and proclaimed the "Third Reich." The Nazi government increased the strength of the German armed forces and sought to overturn the "Versailles Treaty" in order to recover German territory lost at the peace settlement, and to return to the so-called Fatherland German-speaking minorities within the borders of surrounding countries. Later, in 1935, Hitler and the Italian Fascist dictator Benito Mussolini announced a Rome-Berlin alliance – this action formed a two-member team of the so called the "Axis Powers."

Meanwhile, in the Far East, the Japanese - the only major Asian industrial power - coveted the natural resources of China and Southeast Asia, but found their expansion blocked by the European colonial powers or by the United States. Having seized Manchuria in 1931, Japan began a war against China in 1937. Soon thereafter, Germany, Italy, and Japan became allies---making Japan the third member of the so-called Axis Powers.

Furthermore, Mussolini had the immediate war aim of expanding the Italian colonies in North Africa by taking land from the British and French colonies. In addition to their earlier and well-known campaigns in the western desert, the Italians opened an additional front in June 1940 from their East African colonies of Ethiopia, Italian Somaliland, and Eritrea – a country of northeast Africa boarding on the Red Sea.

While this was going on, the British Army had long been in Egypt "protecting" the Suez Canal. The British had been there since 1882 when an expeditionary force was dispatched to Cairo to crush a revolt. While this was meant to be a temporary intervention, British troops stayed in Egypt, this marking the beginning of British occupation and the virtual inclusion of Egypt within the realm and added creditability to the old claim of "the sun never sets on the British Empire!"

Later and in deference to growing nationalism, the UK unilaterally declared Egyptian independence in 1922; however, British influence continued to dominate Egypt's political life and fostered fiscal, administrative, military and governmental reforms. In the mid-1930s, the headquarters of the Royal Navy's Mediterranean Fleet were moved from Malta to Alexandria, Egypt as part of the big plan.

Although Egypt was technically neutral, Cairo soon became a major military base for the British forces leading up to World War II. This was because of a 1936 treaty by which the United Kingdom maintained that it had the right to station troops on Egyptian soil in order to protect the Suez Canal. The use of this canal allowed for a reduced time to be cut for journeys taken from Europe to the Far East. If Britain controlled the Suez, then Nazi Germany and the other Axis powers would not be permitted to use it.

By the start of 1941, the Italian army had been all but beaten and Hitler had to send German troops to North Africa to clear out British troops. The German force was led by Erwin Rommel – the "Desert Fox." Rommel became the principal iconic Axis field commander in North Africa, although the bulk of his forces under his command at this time consisted of Italian troops.

The Italian army attacked the British and Commonwealth troops in Egypt, but they were temporarily driven back until Germany reinforced them. Seesaw battles back and forth across the North African desert between Rommel's Afrika Korps and the Eighth Army came to a brief halt with the British Commonwealth victory at the Second Battle of El Alamein. In March 1941, however, Rommel attacked the British in Libya and by May 1941, they had been pushed back into Egypt and only Tobruk held out against the "Desert Fox".

In the meantime, in the United States things were moving in secret toward the eastern seaboard. Rails and highways hummed with endless possessions of military equipment including tanks, halftracks, field cannons, and jeeps, all covered with their drab-green paint, moved eastward without much notice or comment amongst the civilian population. For weeks'

carload by carload and trainload by
trainload of equipment, supplies, and
military personnel rolled eastward in
secret. Nobody knew what was going on…it
was all done in secret; and, the secret was
being kept.

Elsewhere, on the west coast of the
U.S. and being conducted in secret and in
the middle of the southeastern California's
Mojave Desert-- a bleak, inhospitable,
remote, vast expanse of cactus, scrub and
sand where temperatures ranged from
below freezing to 120 in the shade, where
there was little water and vegetation, other
things were happening. In a secluded area
where dust storms could blind men and
cloudbursts were frequent, military
operations were being conducted inside an
area where elevation ranged from the
desert floor to 7,000 feet above sea level.

It was here in early March of 1942,
that General George S. Patton, [52] the
commander of the Army's First Corps and
his staff had received Top Secret Orders
from the War Department to locate,
established a command, and train troops
for desert warfare. The Army's rationale
was that American forces would eventually
be required to fight the German enemy in
North Africa.

Even while the supplies and military
personnel poured into the awaiting
transport ships in harbors of cities like
Baltimore, New York, Charleston and
Norfolk and the docks swelled high with
American goods of war, across the Atlantic
British vast preparations were underway

also; factories were tooling-up and men were also getting ready for war. Everything being done under the cloak of secrecy.

All this was going on while the free-press of the world was shouting for the opening of a second front against Germany. Little did they know that troops were already pouring into the transport ships from all over the free-world--- American troops, British troops, Canadian troops, Australian troops, Norwegian, Belgian, and Free-French troops--- representing men and material of the united nations gathering for an attack. But the common Soldier, Sailor, and Marine, and even their Officers didn't know where or when any action would occur...it was a secret!

One by one the over-loaded and bulging ships crept out from the harbors of England and the United States under the cover of darkness and into the Atlantic Ocean without any announced destination to the troops, and operating under sealed and secret orders with only a such-and-such longitude and latitude that had been provided only to the skippers of the ships for a preset rendezvous point somewhere out in the Atlantic.

Then suddenly, there were ships, ships everywhere, as far as the eye could see; all kinds of ships: freighters, transports, an ocean liner, destroyers, carriers, battleships, torpedo-boats, and cruisers---the greatest armada of ships the world had ever seen being readied for an unknown destination for battle.

It was just two weeks after Pearl Harbor when President Roosevelt had planned this vast, secret naval operation, and Prime Minister Churchill had vigorously endorsed it, and in those dark days of 1941 the two allied leaders discussed their strategy. To General George Marshall had gone the job of preparing the operations, and in April, while in England, he had received the final approval of the Prime Minister.

In the meantime, Lt. General Eisenhower, as commander of the new European Theater, was selected for the overall execution of the secret plan, while General Mark Clark was responsible for the training of U.S. Troops who had arrived in England. According to Studs Terkel's written account that was published later in book format... this was the start of "The Good War" [11].

However, it must be noted here that several factors had to have been on the minds of the General Eisenhower and the other senior military men in the field who were responsible for executing the battle plan. First, given the secret plan and assignment to invade North Africa only at the end of July 1942, the U.S. Army faced enormous logistical and training difficulties in meeting a target date in November of the same year.

Second, the troops had had little training in amphibious warfare, landing craft were few and obsolete, and much equipment was inferior to that of the Axis forces. Thirdly, so few U.S. troops were available in England that troops for any proposed landing had to be shipped direct from the United States, one of history's longest sea voyages preceding any amphibious assault.

Furthermore, in selecting beaches for the invasion, U.S. planners had insisted upon a landing on the Atlantic coast of Morocco lest the Germans seal the Strait of Gibraltar and cut off support to forces put ashore on the Mediterranean coast. The trade-off was because both troops and shipping were limited; any landing on the Atlantic coast restricted the number and size of landings possible inside the Mediterranean.

On the other hand, although a landing farther east into Tunisia was desirable, due to the vast overland distances from the Atlantic coast to Tunis was more than a thousand miles, the proximity of Axis aircraft on Sicily and Sardinia made that proposal too perilous.

Regardless, ten long months after its formation, the massive convoy slowly nosed its way in silence towards their rendezvous point off the Atlantic Coast and near the Straits of Gibraltar. Only the few "Top Brass" knew where they were bound and what was in store for the hundreds of now impatiently awaiting men who had routinely day after day fell in for inspection of their weapons and battle gear aboard the overloaded ships in preparation for the yet unannounced battleground.

Some wrote letters home, shared pictures of love ones, a few played cards, while others took part in physical exercises aboard the crowded ships to stay in physical shape. But, because of the suspense and anticipation, they all felt in their gut that a great battle was on the horizon.

Eastward from America and southward from England, the greatest armada of ships and men ever assembled near Africa lie waiting for the final orders for movement and a call to action into battle. Ultimately, and in spite of the scuttlebutt, the word came down and a specific movement of the vast number of ships began. Some went southward along the coast of Morocco, while others tracked silently into the Mediterranean, along the northern coast North Africa to the beaches off Oran, Algeria.

Once the success of these proposed landings was assured in the minds of the Top Brass, and the troops were on station and in their designated staging areas, they all waited for the signal for the simultaneous attack to commence.

Then, like the dropping of the gauntlet, some fifteen miles off the coast of Casablanca, aircraft took off from their carriers, landing craft hovered along-side larger troop carrying ships in preparation to receive the men who were climbing down rope-ladders, and the sound of distant gunfire could be heard from the Vichy French on shore.

The long-awaited battle in the opening of the Second Front to confront Germany was now underway. At this same hour, British troops, under the Command of General Montgomery were disembarking ships and making ready for landings along the coast of Algeria. A convoy was to put ashore containing small contingents of British troops to seize ports in eastern Algeria while a ground column headed for Tunisia in a race to get there before the Germans could move in.

As noted below under "Operation Torch," not everything went well during the invasion [51,52].

After soundly defeating an Axis attack, Montgomery's Eighth Army on 23 October 1942 auspiciously opened an offensive at El 'Alamein, there to score a victory that was to be a turning point in British fortunes.

Two weeks later and before dawn on 8 November 1942, the Allies attempted to land the largest amphibious operations that had ever been undertaken in the history of warfare. A naval task force consisting of five aircraft carriers, led by *USS Ranger* (CV-4), plus four *Sangamon* Class escort carriers (ACVs), three battleships, seven cruisers, 38 destroyers, and various other support vessels were dispatched to the western coast of Morocco to lead the attack [50,51].

Green American soldiers waded through the rough surf on three Moroccan beaches, but not without serious problems during their first taste of real battle. The U.S. Navy amphibious landings, historically extremely complicated and requiring much coordination for success even under ideal conditions, were all begun within an hour of each other, were unprecedented in scale, and they began in total darkness near unfamiliar shores.

After several mechanical mishaps with the landing craft, disorientation by both Boatsmates and Coxswain aboard the landing craft during the predawn maneuvers, and fighting the unrelenting rough sea, the first group of green, U.S. Army and Marine troops landed at Safi, the second at Fedala, and the third group came ashore at Mehedia Beach south of Port Lyautey. Within a large horseshoe bend of the meandering flow of the *Sebou River* is Port Lyautey (now called Kenitra) located about five miles inland from where this river empties into the Atlantic Ocean.

At Port Lyautey, the Destroyer *USS Dallas*, (DD199), a Clemson-class four piper, came up the Sebou River, silenced the shore batteries with its big guns and landed an Army Raider team which in turn captured the airfield [50,52].

An interesting and little known fact is that a Moroccan river pilot by the name of Rene Malavergne, who had been imprisoned by the Vichy government in Morocco, had escaped and helped guide the *USS Dallas* up the Sebou that early morning. There are several published accounts of the battle that occurred during the capture of this important airfield during early phases of WW II [50,52,55, 69].

These troops were the vanguard for a series of operations that eventually involved more than a million of their

British compatriots who were in action in the Mediterranean area in Oran and Algiers in northern Algeria.

Despite Hitler warnings that Vichy France would suffer greatly if they did not resist the Allied invasion, the French leader in Algiers, Admiral Jean Darlan, agreed to a cease-fire on 11 Nov 1942. Most French units followed Darlan's lead, but Pétain tried to rescind Darlan's order, and some Vichy soldiers joined German units in Tunisia.

In spite of all the problems, American troops in their first taste of battle had made many mistakes. Training, equipment, and leadership had failed in many instances to meet the requirements of the battlefield, but the lessons were clear and pointed to nothing that time might not correct. More important was the experience gained, both in battle and in logistical support.

Important too was the fact the Allies at last had gained the initiative and the invasions were declared a complete success. Allied troop who landed in Vichy controlled Morocco, later linked up with the Eighth Army and succeeded in driving the "*Axis*" from the continent.

A second example of a major "Diplomatic Blunder" I would emphasize at this juncture is that even though the United States never officially indorsed the French Protectorate in Morocco, it gave tacit recognition, claimed the protection of its authority, and proclaimed legal justification for its first involvement in

North Africa in 1940, and continued to conduct business under this same code of conduct over the next quarter century.

As was reported by Blair [55], and, as I suggest here: Even before the invasion into North Africa at the start of WW II, President Roosevelt was seduced by Churchill to follow British strategy and to go along with his policy regardless of the President's personal convictions on colonization.

The British felt that a strong central French authority was necessary to ensure the tranquility of North Africa during and after the invasion [52,55,69]. However, the jury is still out regarding the effect of Roosevelt's health at the time. Did he suffer from any serious ailments that could have affected his judgment as the nation became imperiled by WW II?

Also, following the bombing at Pearl Harbor in 1941, most of America's military energy was directed at the Japanese in the Pacific. With increased pressure from Russia and England for a serious attempt to engage Hitler in the west in early 1942, the Second World War had reached a turning point. The Allies were desperate to slow the German eastward advances in Egypt and the Soviet Union.

As already stated above, the British were busy battling Erwin Rommel and his Afrika Korps. Stalin was demanding that the western Allies open up a second front in Europe to relieve the pressure on the Red Army. Everything about the War was bad---things were going to hell in a handbasket. To top it off, all the Allies were as dependent on supplies and equipment from the U.S. as American troops were... merchant ships were being loaded in all American ports, mustering in the Gulf of Mexico and in ports along both oceans, forming convoys as Nazi U-boats stood ready to attack ... and attack they did in Wolf-packs [49].

Prime Minister Winston Churchill suggested an invasion of North Africa, followed by an invasion of Europe in 1943.

Roosevelt agreed to support our British ally and it was decided that an invasion of North Africa would be staged. () The Anglo-American force was to seize Morocco and Algeria, which were controlled by Vichy France, then push eastward to meet the British 8th Army, which was commanded by General Montgomery

However, before America's invasion onto foreign soil one should know something of the lay of the land. Geographically, Morocco contains a central backbone of mountains, but it is flanked by deserts and plains. The Atlas chain, beginning south of Marrakech, separates that city and the coastal plain from the desert country to the south and east.

The southern part of this long chain is the High Atlas, and even in summer there is snow on some peaks. From Marrakech, the chain turns northeast and becomes the Middle Atlas that extends into Algeria. A narrow corridor, known as the Taza Gap, links the Atlantic plains with Algeria and the rest of northern Africa.

Further north another smaller chain, the Rif Mountains, runs parallel with the Mediterranean coastline ending near the city of Tetouan. These mountains enclose the Atlantic plains like a wall, and catch the rainfall brought in by the prevailing westerly winds from the Atlantic during the winter months.

All the main rivers run westwards into the Atlantic; only the *Moulouya* River flows northwards into the Mediterranean Sea. Only the *Sebou* and the *Oum er Rbia* carry a large amount of water for most of the year.

The history of the undertow, winds, and water flow that produces an undercurrent along the western coast of Morocco has been known to be notoriously dangerous to swimming and to the use of small boats. With this picture of the topography the ocean currents in mind, one can visualize what may happen during an invasion.

Safi is now the main fishing port for the country's sardine industry, and used for exporting phosphates, textiles and ceramics. Fedala, now named Mohammedia, is a port city northeast of Casablanca, and years earlier this harbor was frequented in the 14th and 15th centuries by merchant ships from Europe seeking cereals and dried fruits.

III. The Aftermath of the Invasion:

Not unlike our other military invasions, including our recent invasion of Iraq in 2003, the reestablishment of civil authority proved to be the most demanding approach and required unique diplomatic skill in WW II. A review of these events that transpired post invasion has revealed some interesting findings listed below. Little did anyone suspect that following the invasion and military action, a major war of words between the generals would result and long prevail!

As revealed by David Irving [70], the war between the generals continued long after the guns had fallen still, especially between Patton, Rommel, Eisenhower, and Montgomery; the four major and most flamboyant, controversial and influential commanders.

Also, as revealed in the third "Private Agreement," from notes that were published by Funk, [71] and are said to have been released to the press from the Casablanca Conference in early 1943, reports showed that a great deal of time was being devoted to discussions of future invasions and of a "unconditional surrender;" but not many news stories carried details of these negotiations [55,69,70].

There was little released regarding the tenor of the negotiations or the policies pursued by President Roosevelt, or the differences of opinion between the president and Churchill regarding General de Gaulle. But we do know that promises had been made to General Henri Giraud by Robert Murphy, the American diplomat who had been in contact with the French resistance groups in North Africa for months prior to the invasion [55,69,70].

Admiral Darlan had been appointed leader of French North Africa by General Dwight D. Eisenhower, angering General Charles De Gaulle. General Darlan was later killed by a Free French assassin on the afternoon of 24 December 1942. Regardless, the understanding was that French sovereignty would be restored in Morocco after the Invasion. Therefore, the Darlan-Clark Agreement and the Giraud-Murphy correspondence secured French control of Morocco's infrastructure, but allowed Allied forces to use it and give them extraterritorial privilege while there [66,69,70].

The U.S. official objective in Morocco was said to be short-term and military, not political. It was to secure French Morocco quickly and to establish a striking force in the French area of Morocco capable of ensuing control of the Strait of Gibraltar by moving into Spanish Morocco, and with the view of occupying Tunisia [52,54,55].

The possibility of intervention by Spain was still considered a real threat. After consolidating their strength in French territory, the Allies, with General George Patton in charge, struck into Tunisia, nearly capturing Tunis before a German counterattack drove them back. In the East, Montgomery drove Rommel's retreating army back to Tunisia [52].

The two Allied armies, converging on Tunisia, met stiff German resistance, but on May 7 the British took Tunis and by May 13 the Axis forces in Tunisia had surrendered, leaving North Africa under complete Allied control. This paved the way for the Allied invasions of Sicily and Italy, finally opening up the second European front desired by Churchill and Stalin [55].

Prostitution and "black market" activities began in Port Lyautey soon after the arrival of the U.S. invasion forces in 1942 and the subsequent social and economic impact of the military upon the local community was immediate [55].

After the invasion, the U.S. Army took control of the French military base at Port Lyautey and it was used by United States military forces during WW II until 15 February 1943, at which time it passed to the U.S. Navy; and, major improvements were made and it was expanded to a U.S. Naval Air Station by1953.

Thereafter, it provided a training, support and repair facility for the US Naval Communications Stations in Bouknadel and Sidi Yahia as well as a maintenance area for the many squadrons of anti-submarine aircraft from bases in the United States who were on patrol over the Atlantic Ocean and the entire Mediterranean Sea.

The status of the military bases in Morocco during the Cold War was one of necessity for the United States, and all operational dialogs about of the bases were being made with the French Protectorate, ignoring the sultan's efforts to initiate some discussions. After independence from France in 1956, diplomatic relations between Morocco and France was in a state of flux [55].

Furthermore, serious direct diplomatic discussions between the U.S. and Morocco failed to ever materialize during the Eisenhower administration; even though several Moroccan cities had been the setting numerous times for earlier meetings with British Prime Minister Churchill and FDR. One example was on 25 November 1957, when Mohammad V tried to get some discussions going when he used the metaphor "A bridge between the East and West" following his last visit with President Eisenhower [55,70].

*****

Addendum E "

148.Memorandum of Conversation;

Washington, 27 March 1963; 4:30 p.m.

SUBJECT: American Bases in Morocco [72].

PARTICIPANTS: His Majesty King Hassan II of Morocco; President Kennedy; Mr. Edmund Glenn, Interpreter

The President brought up the subject of the American bases. He mentioned that the U.S. is prepared to withdraw from the three air bases, as this had undoubtedly been communicated to His Majesty by the American Ambassador. We would desire, however, to keep the telecommunications facilities of the naval base at Kenitra. What are the King's ideas on the subject?

The King asked the President for his proposals: The President said that we attached a considerable amount of importance to the telecommunications base at Kenitra, as there are no other facilities easily available in that part of the world and as the installation had been quite costly. There might be a possibility to remove the facilities to Spain, but this would take time and call for special negotiations.

The King said that when he came to the United States in 1960 as head of the Moroccan Delegation to the United Nations, he spent a full day at the Pentagon where he was thoroughly briefed by representatives of American Naval aviation. He was shown also films about the Kenitra facilities and he fully realizes their importance.

At the same time, however, an agreement had been reached between the United States Government and his late Majesty, the King's father, which provided for withdrawal from the bases at the end of 1963. This has a great importance in the eyes of Moroccan public opinion and the King would not wish to appear in any way to have broken an item of his father's will. This is the problem to which a solution needs to be found.

The President stated that our withdrawal from the three air bases would amount to carrying out the agreement mentioned by the King. As for the Naval facility, some arrangements might be found--for example, in the area of command--which would make American presence at that base less conspicuous, but which would allow us to continue using the facilities for a period of time, until they could be phased out.

The King asked for how long would the U.S. wish to keep its facilities.

The President said for as long as the Moroccans would have us.

The King asked what would be the minimum.

The President suggested that five years might be the minimum. The President further said that an arrangement as to the command structure of the bases might be sought in connection with some economic programs and also with some help to the Moroccan Navy which, although not necessarily directly tied to the Kenitra base, would nevertheless be to the advantage of that Navy.

The King said that while he understood the interest of the United States in that question, what is important in fact are the telecommunications facilities, which are needed by the United States to cover the Atlantic and even part of the Pacific. Under those circumstances, it would be useful to seek some sort of arrangement, if this were to prove possible." (Everything taken from Department of State Memorandum #148).

As noted, the United States had agreed to leave as of December 1959, and the Air Force was to be out of Morocco in the fall of 1963. Strategic Air Command (SAC) felt the Moroccan bases were much less critical and unnecessary for our world-wide security with the long-range use of the B-52 bombers. And, with the completion of an agreement in 1959, the U.S. Navy had also planned to eventually move to the Spanish base at Rota, Spain.

I later learned that four years before the Cuban missile crisis erupted over Soviet deployment of nuclear weapons in Cuba, the U.S. had nuclear bombs stored in Morocco and in 41 other locations worldwide. The locations included 14 bases on the territories of six foreign countries: Canada, Greenland, Denmark, Japan, Spain, and the United Kingdom [55].

These two superpowers came away from this experience heading in opposite strategic directions. The Soviets, determined not to be humiliated again, pushed forward their nuclear buildup with unrelenting vigor. The U.S., in contrast, cut back building its forces and nuclear programs. This was because President Kennedy and the policymakers, and rightly so, had doubts about strategic superiority. Kennedy understood the need for military strength, but he also saw it as being too provocative.

*****

Addendum F

This is additional confirmation of the ways in which unfavorable Cold War publicity concerns shaped American humanitarian efforts in Morocco. By revisiting and examining responses to the 1959 cooking oil adulteration in light of other work [73,74] on American Cold War public relations, as well as the work of analysts of more recent 'disaster diplomacy,' [53,55,66] we get a feel for diplomacy.

The Cold War provided an incentive for American disaster aid – but it also distorted that aid, as American policy prioritized immediate, visible aid over long-term relief efforts. An example being the 1959 tri-ortho-cresyl phosphate (TCP) poisoning, which paralyzed 10,000 people [73, 74].

Fears that generosity would imply culpability for the incident, which originated with the sale of a neurotoxic surplus substances from a former U.S. Air Force SAC base established without permission from the Moroccan government. However, a new and even greater calamity, the earthquake at Agadir, transformed the calculus of American disaster assistance in Morocco, liberating American officials to respond more effectively to the needs of the toxic oil victims. For the historian, the political calculations shaping the US response to the 1959 oil poisoning in Morocco illuminate the dynamics of Cold War humanitarianism; for the disaster response

275

analyst, this case study demonstrates how disaster diplomacy can affect disaster response [55,73,74].

In the States during the 1930's, thousands of cases of muscle pain, weakness of upper and lower extremities, and minimal sensory impairment occurred in the United States. The neurotoxic illness was caused by the consumption of an adulterated Jamaica ginger extract ("Jake"), an illicit beverage then popularly used in the southern and Midwestern United States to circumvent prohibition statutes. The additive TCP caused severe, only partially reversible damage to the spinal cord and peripheral nervous tissue. Victims with resultant gait impairment, sometimes permanent, were said to have the "Jake Leg" or "Jake Walk." Over a dozen musical recordings were made by Blues and Country artists referring to Jake or Jake-induced infirmity in their song lyrics.

These musical references revealed cultural familiarity with Jake, and the later, post-epidemic performances reflect a whimsical, even cynical, cultural attitude that those with "Jake Leg" were suffering the wages of sin and should not be regarded as objects of pity or sympathy.

*****

REFERENCES

1). Clemens, S.L.: Author's Notes Under the pseudonym of Mark Twain.

2). Amis, Sir Kingsley: *Amis Memoirs*, Penguin Press, 1992.

3). Shackelford, L. & Weinberg, B.: *Our Appalachia. An Oral History*. U. of Kentucky Press, 1988.

4). Kleber, J.E.: *The Kentucky Encyclopedia.* U. of Kentucky Press, 1992.

5). Montgomery, M.: *How Scot-Irish is our English?* J. of East TN. History. 67:17-18, 1995.

6). Adams, L.E.: *"Fried Potatoes, Mustard Greens, Fat Back, Soup Beans, and Cornbread---Retracing the Vanishing Footprints of Our Appalachian Ancestors."* 1st Books, Bloomington, IN. 2004.

7). Adams, L.E.: *"Bandits, Farmers, Military Leaders, Patriots, Politicians, and Prophets. Retracing the Vanishing Footprints of Our Ancestors.* AuthorHouse, Bloomington, IN & U.K., 2007.

8). Cox, C. R.: *"Appalachia Crossroads. Descendants of Hezekiah Sellards. (Father of Jenny Wiley). Vol. 1."* Gateway Press, Inc., Baltimore, 1977.

9). Vance, J.: *Hillbilly Elegy. Memoir of a family and culture in Crisis.* HarperCollins, N.Y., N.Y., 2016.

10). Terkel, S.: *Hard Times. An Oral History of the Great Depression.* Pantheon Books, N.Y., N.Y., 1970.

11). Terkel, S.: *The Good War.* Pantheon Books, N.Y., N.Y., 1984.

12). Brose, D. & Greber, N.: *Hopewell Archaeology. The Chillicothe Conference.* The Kent State U. Press, Kent, Oh.1979.

13). Cavender, A.: *Folk Medicine in Southern Appalachia.* The U. of North Carolina Press, 2003.

14). *A to Z of the Ancient World.* 2008 International Masters Publishers AB. Printed in China.

15), Krauss, L.M.: *Faith and Foolishness.* Scientific American. 303:36, August 2010.

16). Vance, E.: *Mind over Matter.* National Geographic. 230: 30-55, 2016.

17). Abramson, J.: *Overdosed America. The broken promise of American medicine.* HarperCollins, N.Y., N.Y., 2004.

18). Jaret, P.: *The Antibiotics Emergency.* AARP Bulletin, November 2016.

19). Williamson, K.: *The White Ghetto. In Appalachia, the country is beautiful and the society is broken.* National Review, 9 January 2014.

20). Ridgway, M. B.: *The Korean War.* Da Capo Press, Cambridge, MA, 1986.

21). Blair, C.: *The Forgotten War: America in Korea 1950–53.* New York: Doubleday, 1987.

22). Medert, P.F: *Stories from Chillicothe's Past.* 1997, Published by Author.

23). Gieck, J.: *A Photo Album of Ohio's Canal. Era, 1825-1913.* Kent State Press., Kent Oh. 1988.

24). Campbell, M.J.: *Enlisted Naval Aviation Pilots: a legacy of service.* Naval Aviation News. Nov-Dec., 2003.

25). Kelly, H. & Riley, W.: *Enlisted Naval Aviation Pilots.* Turner Publishing Company, 1997.

26). *The Sullivan Brothers and the Assignment of Family Members to U.S. Navy Ships.* Dept. of the Navy, Naval Historical Center, Washington, DC 20374-5060.

27). Lawless, D. K. 1953. *A rapid permanent-mount stain technique for the diagnosis of intestinal protozoa.* Am. J. Trop. Med. Hyg. 2:1137-1138.

28). Sapero, J. & Lawless, D.K.: *The "MIF' stain-preservation technique for the identification of intestinal protozoa.* Am. J. Trop. Med. Hyg. 2: 613-619, 1953.

29). Kuntz, R. E., Lawless, D. K., & Langbehn, H. R. *Intestinal protozoa and helminths in the peoples of western (Anatolia) Turkey.* Am. J. Trop. Med. Hyg. 7: 298-301, (1958).

30). Hoogstraal H, Huff CG, & Lawless DK. *A malarial parasite of the African elephant shrew, Elephantulus rufescens dundasi.* J Natl Malar Soc.9 (4): 293, 1950.

31). Kuntz, R.E, Malakatis, GM, Lawless, DK, Strome, & CP: *Medical mission to the Yemen, Southwest Arabia 1951. II. A cursory survey of the intestinal protozoa and helminth arasites in the people of the Yemen.* Am J Trop. Med. Hyg., Jan. 2 (1): 13-9, 1953.

32. Kuntz RE, Lawless DK, & Mansour NS: *A cursory survey of the intestinal parasites in relatives living in Southwest Sudan.* Am J Trop Med Hyg? Sep. 4(5):895-900, 1955.

33). Lawless, D K, Kuntz, R E, and et al.: *Amoebiasis.* Am. J. Trop. Med. Hyg. 5, 1010, 1956.

34). Kuntz RE, Lawless DK, & Strome CP: *Intestinal parasites in an Egyptian village of the Nile Valley with emphasis on the protozoa.* Am J Trop Med Hyg? Nov. 5 (6):1010-4, 1956.

35). Kuntz, R E, Lawless, DK, et al.: *Intestinal protozoa and helminths in the peoples of Egypt living in different type localities.* Am. J. Trop. Med. Hyg., 7, 630, 1958.

36). Kuntz, R. E., Lawless, D. K., & Langbehn, H. R.: *Intestinal protozoa and helminthes in the peoples of western (Anatolia) Turkey.* Am. J. Trop. Med. Hyg. 7: 298-301, 1958.

37). Kuntz, R.E. & Lawless, D.K.: *Acquisition of intestinal protozoa and helminthes by young children in a typical village of Lower Egypt.* Am J Trop Med Hyg? Jul; 7(4):353-7, 1958.

38). Kuntz, R.E., Lawless, DK, Malakatis, GM: *Intestinal protozoans and helminths in Americans residing in southern Taiwan (Formosa).* Am. J. Trop. Med. Hyg. Jan; 8 (1):63-6, 1959.

39). Kuntz RE & Lawless DK: *Intestinal protozoans and helminths in the indigenous population and employees associated with a Naval Air Station in the Philippines.* Mil. Med.125: 561-6, 1960.

40). Beye, HK. & Lawless, DK: *Viability of microfilariae of Wuchereria bancrofti during prolonged storage at-25 degrees C.* Exp. Parasitol. Nov., 11: 319-22, 1961.

41). Hill, G. II, Knight, V, Coatney, GR, & Lawless DK: *Vivax malaria complicated by aphasia and hemiparesis.* Arch Intern Med. Dec; 112 (6):863-8, 1963.

42). Kuntz, R. & Lawless, D.K.: *Intestinal parasites of peoples of Taiwan. Intestinal parasites of aborigines (Yami) of Lan Yu (Orchid Island). Taiwan Yi Xue Hui Za Zhi.* Jun 28; 65(6): 287-93, 1966.

43). Lawless D.K. & Knight V.: *Human infection with Entamoeba polecki: report of four cases.* Am J Trop Med Hyg. Sep.15 (5):701-4, 1966.

44). Adams LE: *Medical Frontier.* U.S. Navy Medical Newsletter, Vol. 45, No 5, 1965.

45). Pace, E.: *James J. Humes Dies at 74; Did Autopsy on Kennedy.* New York Times. 12 May, 1999.

46). Adams, L.E.: *The Adams Chronicles. Volume II* (In press).

47). Adams, L.E.: *Medical Frontier.* U.S. Navy Medical Newsletter, Vol. 45, No 5, 1965.

48). Lilius, A.: *Turbulent Tangier.* Elek Books, 1956.

49. Blumenson, M.: *Patton: The Man behind the Legend 1885-1945.* New York: William Morrow and Company Inc., 1985.

50). Comtois, P.: "*First Fire of Operation Torch,*" WW II Magazine. Volume II, Issue 4, November, 1996.

51). Ewing, P.: *Destroyer's WW II mission snared N. African airstrip.* Deputy News Editor, Navy Times.

52). Patton, G.S., Jr.: *War as I Knew It.* Bantam Books, New York, 1947.

53). Adams, C.: *Inside the Cold War; a Cold Warrior's Reflections,* Air University Press. 2nd Printing 2004; 3rd Printing 2005, 1999.

54). Buchanan, R.: *The United States and WW II.* New York: Harper & Row Publishers, 2002.

55). Blair, L.B.: *Western Window in the Arab World.* The University of Texas Press. Austin & London, 1970.

56). Hibbard, A.: *Paul Bowles, Magic of Morocco.* Cadmus Editions, California, 2004.

57). Adams, L.E: *An Epidemiological Survey of Rabies in Morocco.* J. Amer. Med Tech. 29:5, 1967.

58). Adams, L.E: *Rabies in the United States. A Review of the Literature and the Efficacy of Post-Exposure Treatment.* J. Am. Med. Tech. 33:137-146, 1971.

59). Ashford, D.: *Political Change in Morocco.* The Princeton University Press, 1964.

60). Fremont-Barnes, G.: "Outbreak." *The Wars of the Barbary Pirates: To the Shores of Tripoli: The Birth of the US Navy and Marines.* Osprey Publishing, 2006.

61). Maxwell, G.: *Lords of the Atlas. Adventure, Mystery, and Intrigue in Morocco, 1893-1956.* The Lyons Press, Guilford, CT 06437, 2000.

62). Fage, J.: *A History of Africa.* Routledge, London, England, 1995.

63). Nelson, H.: *Morocco, a country study.* Foreign Area Studies. The American University, Washington, DC, 1985.

64). Broder, J.: *Tangier: tales of pirates, diplomacy, and espionage frame America's liaison with an exotic city.* Smithsonian. 29, No.4, pages 90-101, Washington, D.C., 1998.

65). Dozy, R.: *The History of the Almohades.* Leiden: 1881.

66). Blair, L.: *Amateurs in Diplomacy: The American Vice Consuls in North Africa 1941-1943.* John Wiley & Sons, 1973.

67). London, J.E.: *Victory in Tripoli: How America's War with the Barbary Pirates Established the U.S. Navy and Shaped a Nation.* John Wiley & Sons, Inc., NJ, 2005.

68). Defoe, D.: *Robinson Crusoe.* Published by Grosset & Dunlap, 1946.

69). Murphy, R.: *Diplomat Among Warriors.* Doubleday & Co., Garden City, NJ, 1965.

70). Irving, D.: *The War Between the Generals. Inside the Allied High Command.* Penguin Books, 1981.

71). Funk, A.L.: *Charles de Gaulle: The Crucial Years, 1943-1944.* U. of Oklahoma Press. Norman, OK, 1959.

72). Foreign Relations, 1961-1963, Africa (Morocco) # 108. *Memorandum from Secretary of State Rusk to President Kennedy.* Released by the Office of the Historian, U.S. Department of State, Wash. DC.

73). Smith, H.V. & Spalding, J.M.K: *Outbreak of paralysis in Morocco due to ortfto-cresyl phosphate poisoning.* Lancet 2, 1019, 1959.

74). Segalle, S.: *The Moroccan Oil Poising and Cold War Disaster Diplomacy.* J. North African Studies. 17: 315, 2012.

75), Tacala, M.: The U.S. Navy Hospital Corps: A Century of Tradition, Valor, and Sacrifice. WWW.Corpsman.com.

*****

Printed in the United States
By Bookmasters